AND HIS MESSAGE

From its Publication Department, Kolkata

SWAMI VIVEKANANDA

Advaita Ashrama
(Publication Department)
5 Dehi Entally Road
Kolkata 700 014

Published by
Swami Mumukshananda
President, Advaita Ashrama
Mayavati, Champawat, Himalayas
from its Publication Department, Kolkata
Email: advaita@vsnl.com
Website: www.advaitaonline.com

© *All Rights Reserved*
Ninth Impression, May 2005
3M3C

ISBN 81-7505-074-8

Printed in India at
Trio Process
Kolkata 700 014

PREFACE
TO THE FIRST REPRINT

The first edition of *Ramakrishna and His Message* which presents between two covers Swami Vivekananda's reminiscences and reflections concerning his Master, Sri Ramakrishna, was published by the Belur Math.

In order to ensure its larger circulation we are now bringing out the first reprint of this valuable publication at the request of the original publisher.

Advaita Ashrama   The Publisher
Mayavati, Almora,
Himalayas,
February 16, 1972

PREFACE TO THE FIRST EDITION

Once Swami Vivekananda was asked to write a biography of Sri Ramakrishna. The request embarrassed Swamiji, and he remarked: 'Shall I make the image of a monkey, trying to manufacture that of Shiva?' And this he said, after his return from the West when he was world famous as an orator and writer. In spite of expressing such a difficulty, Swamiji did speak and write about Sri Ramakrishna. And when we recall Sri Ramakrishna's high estimation of his Narendranath, what the disciple said about the Master is of great consequence.

The reminiscences and profound reflections of Swamiji concerning his beloved Master are scattered throughout the eight volumes of *The Complete Works of Swami Vivekananda* and in other literature. To bring them together in one place, as has been done in this book, obviously serves a real need. It is worth adding, however, that Vivekananda's own life was, as it were, Ramakrishna himself in action. Not only in Swamiji's explicit utterances, but implicitly all through his *Complete Works* Sri Ramakrishna is present, for the mind of the disciple was not other than that of the Master.

The present book, it is hoped, will set at rest any doubt about Swamiji's correct representation of his Master.

Belur Math   The Publisher
Sri Ramakrishna's Birthday
27 February 1971

CONTENTS

CONTENTS

RAMAKRISHNA AND HIS MESSAGE

Ramakrishna Paramahamsa came for the good of the world. Call him a man, or God, or an Incarnation, just as you please. Accept him each in your own light. He who will bow before him will be converted into purest gold that very moment. Go with this message from door to door. *Spread only what he came to teach. Never mind his name— it will spread of itself.* (VI. 266, 274)

RAMAKRISHNA'S LIFE

'Whenever virtue subsides and vice prevails, I come down to help mankind,' declares Krishna, in the *Bhagavad Gita*. Whenever this world of ours, on account of growth, on account of added circumstances, requires a new adjustment, a wave of power comes. I am going to present before you the life of one man who has put in motion such a wave in India.

It was while reforms of various kinds were being inaugurated in India that a child was born of poor Brahmin parents on the eighteenth of February 1836, in one of the remote villages of Bengal. The father and mother were very orthodox people. The life of a really orthodox Brahmin is one of continuous renunciation. Very poor they were, and yet many a time the mother would starve herself a whole day to help a poor man. Of them this child was born; and he was a peculiar child from very boyhood. He remembered his past from his birth and was conscious for what purpose he came into the world, and every power was devoted to the fulfilment of that purpose.

While he was quite young, his father died; and the boy was sent to school. A Brahmin's boy must go to school; the caste restricts him to a learned profession only. The boy was peculiar, as I have said, and he gathered this moral out of it [a discussion of some professors]: 'This is the outcome of all their knowledge. Why are they fighting so hard? It is simply for money; the man who can show the highest learning here will get the best pair of cloth, and that is all these people are struggling for. I will not go to school any more.' And he did not; that was the end of his going to school. But this boy had an elder brother, a learned professor, who took him to Calcutta, however, to study with him. After a short time the boy became fully convinced that the aim of all secular learning was mere material advancement, and nothing more, and he resolved to give up study and devote himself solely to the pursuit of spiritual knowledge. The father being dead, the family was very poor; and this boy had to make his own living. He went to a place near Calcutta and became a temple priest.

In the temple was an image of the 'Blissful Mother'. This boy had to conduct the worship morning and evening, and by degrees this one idea filled his mind: 'Is there anything behind this image? Is it true that there is a Mother of Bliss in the universe? Is it true that She lives and guides the universe, or is it all a dream? Is there any reality in religion?'

This idea took possession of the boy and his whole life became concentrated upon that. Day after day he would weep and say: 'Mother, is it true that Thou existest, or is it all poetry? Is the Blissful Mother an imagination of poets and misguided people, or is there such a Reality?'

However, this thought—whether God can be

seen—which was uppermost in his mind gained in strength every day until he could think of nothing else. He could no more conduct the worship properly, could no more attend to the various details in all their minuteness. Often he would forget to place the food-offering before the image, sometimes he would forget to wave the light; at other times he would wave it for hours, and forget everything else.

And that one idea was in his mind every day: 'Is it true that Thou existest, O Mother? Why dost Thou not speak? Art Thou dead?'

At last it became impossible for him to serve in the temple. He left it and entered into a little wood that was near and lived there. About this part of his life, he told me many times that he could not tell when the sun rose or set, or how he lived. He lost all thought of himself and forgot to eat. During this period he was lovingly watched over by a relative who put into his mouth food which he mechanically swallowed.

Days and nights thus passed with the boy. When a whole day would pass, towards the evening, when the peal of bells in the temples, and the voices singing, would reach the wood, it would make the boy very sad, and he would cry: 'Another day is gone in vain, Mother, and Thou hast not come. Another day of this short life has gone, and I have not known the Truth.' In the agony of his soul, sometimes he would rub his face against the ground and weep, and this one prayer burst forth: 'Do Thou manifest Thyself in me, Thou Mother of the

universe! See that I need Thee and nothing else!'
Verily, he wanted to be true to his own ideal. He
had heard that the Mother never came until everything had been given up for Her.

He threw away all the little property he had, and
took a vow that he would never touch money, and
this one idea, 'I will not touch money', became a
part of him. It may appear to be something occult,
but even in after-life when he was sleeping, if I
touched him with a piece of money his hand would
become bent, and his whole body would become,
as it were, paralysed. The other idea that came into
his mind was that lust was the other enemy. Man
is a soul, and soul is sexless, neither man nor woman.
The idea of sex and the idea of money were the two
things, he thought, that prevented him from seeing
the Mother. This whole universe is the manifestation of the Mother, and She lives in every woman's
body. 'Every woman represents the Mother; how
can I think of woman in mere sex relation?' That
was the idea: Every woman was his Mother, he
must bring himself to the state when he would see
nothing but Mother in every woman. And he
carried it out in his life.

This is the tremendous thirst that seizes the
human heart. This divine madness seized the boy.
At that time he had no teacher, nobody to tell him
anything, and every one thought that he was out
of his mind. This is the ordinary condition of things.
If a man throws aside the vanities of the world,
we hear him called mad. But such men are the salt

of the earth. Out of such madness have come the powers that have moved this world of ours, and out of such madness alone will come the powers of the future that are going to move the world.

So days, weeks, months passed in continuous struggle of the soul to arrive at truth. The boy began to see visions, to see wonderful things; the secrets of his nature were beginning to open to him. Veil after veil was, as it were, being taken off. Mother Herself became the teacher and initiated the boy into the truths he sought.

At this time there came to this place a woman of beautiful appearance, learned beyond compare. Later on, this saint used to say about her that she was not learned, but was the embodiment of learning; she was learning itself, in human form. She was a Sannyasini. She came; and when she heard of this boy in the grove, she offered to go and see him; and hers was the first help he received. At once she recognized what his trouble was, and she said to him: 'My son, blessed is the man upon whom such madness comes.' This woman remained near the boy for years, taught him the forms of the religions of India, initiated him into the different practices of Yoga, and, as it were, guided and brought into harmony this tremendous river of spirituality.

Later, there came to the same grove a Sannyasin, one of the begging friars of India, a learned man, a philosopher. He was a peculiar man, he was an idealist. He did not believe that this world existed in reality; and to demonstrate that, he would never go under a roof, he would always live out of doors, in storm and sunshine alike. This man began to teach the boy the philosophy of the Vedas; and he found very soon, to his astonishment, that the pupil was in some respects wiser than the master. He spent several months with the boy, after which he initiated him into the order of Sannyasins, and took his departure.

When as a temple priest his extraordinary worship made people think him deranged in his head, his relatives took him home and married him to a little girl, thinking that that would turn his thoughts and restore the balance of his mind. But he came back and, as we have seen, merged deeper in his madness. The husband had entirely forgotten that he had a wife. In her far off home the girl had heard that her husband had become a religious enthusiast, and that he was even considered insane by many. She resolved to learn the truth for herself, so she set out and walked to the place where her husband was. When at last she stood in her husband's presence, he at once admitted her right to his life, although in India any person, man or woman, who embraces a religious life, is thereby freed from all other obligations. The young man fell at the feet of his wife and said, 'As for me, the Mother has shown me that She resides in every woman, and so I have learnt to look upon every woman as Mother. That is the one idea I can have about you; but if you wish to drag me into the world, as I have been married to you, I am at your service.'

The maiden was a pure and noble soul and was able to understand her husband's aspirations and sympathize with them. She quickly told him that she had no wish to drag him down to a life of worldliness; but that all she desired was to remain near him, to serve him, and to learn of him. She became one of his most devoted disciples, always revering him as a divine being. Thus through his wife's consent the last barrier was removed, and he was free to lead the life he had chosen.

The next desire that seized upon the soul of this man was to know the truth about the various religions. Up to that time he had not known any religion but his own. He found a Mohammedan saint and placed himself under him, he underwent the disciplines prescribed by him and to his astonishment found that when faithfully carried out, these devotional methods led him to the same goal he had already attained. He gathered similar experience from following the true religion of Jesus the Christ. He went to all the sects he could find, and whatever he took up he went into it with his whole heart.

He then set about to learn humility, because he had found that the one idea in all religions is, 'not me, but Thou', and he who says, 'not me', the Lord fills his heart. Now my Master would go to a Pariah and ask to be allowed to clean his house. The Pariah would not permit it; so in the dead of night, when all were sleeping, Ramakrishna would enter the house. He had long hair, and with his hair he would wipe the place, saying, 'Oh, my Mother, make me the servant of the Pariah, make me feel that I am even lower than the Pariah.' 'They worship Me best, who worship My worshippers. These are all My children and your privilege is to serve them'—is the teaching of Hindu scriptures.

This rigorous, unsullied purity came into the life of that man. All the struggles which we have in our lives were past for him. His hard-earned jewels of spirituality, for which he had given three-quarters of his life, were now ready to be given to humanity, and then began his mission: First make character—that is the highest duty you can perform. Know Truth for yourself, and there will be many to whom you can teach it afterwards; they will all come. This was the attitude of my Master. He criticised no one. For years I lived with that man, but never did I hear those lips utter one word of condemnation for any sect. He had the same sympathy for all sects; he had found the harmony between them. People came by thousands to see and hear this wonderful man, who spoke in a *patois*, every word of which was forceful and instinct with light.

He looked just like an ordinary man, with nothing remarkable about him. He used the most simple language, and I thought, 'Can this man be a great teacher?'—crept near to him and asked him the question which I had been asking others all my life: 'Do you believe in God, Sir?' 'Yes'. 'How?' 'Because I see Him just as I see you here, only in a much intenser sense.' That impressed me at once. For the first time I found a man who dared to say that he saw God, that religion was a reality, to be felt, to be sensed in an infinitely more intense way than we can sense the world. I began to go to that man, day after day, and I actually saw that religion could be given. One touch, one glance, can change a whole life.

I learnt from my Master that the religions of the world are not contradictory or antagonistic. They are but various phases of one eternal religion.... In one man, religion is manifesting itself as intense activity, as work. In another, it is manifesting itself as intense devotion, in yet another, as mysticism, in others as philosophy, and so forth. It is wrong when we say to others, 'Your methods are not right'. Do not try to disturb the faith of any man.

The first part of my Master's life was spent in acquiring spirituality, and the remaining years in distributing it. Men came in crowds to hear him, and he would talk twenty hours in the twenty-four, and that not for one day, but for months and months, until at last the body broke down under the pressure of this tremendous strain. His intense love for mankind would not let him refuse to help even the humblest of the thousands who sought his aid. Gradually there developed a vital throat disorder, and yet he could not be persuaded to refrain from these exertions. As soon as he heard that

2

people were asking to see him, he would insist upon having them admitted, and would answer all their questions. When expostulated with, he replied, 'I do not care. I will give up twenty thousand such bodies to help one man.' There was no rest for him. 'While I can speak, I must teach them,' he would say, and he was as good as his word.

One day, he told us that he would lay down the body that day, and repeating the most sacred word of the Vedas he entered into Samadhi and passed away.

(Compiled from the lecture 'My Master': IV 154-87)

THE MASTER AND HIS MESSAGE

THE MASTER

The time was ripe for one to be born, who in one body would have the brilliant intellect of Shankara and the wonderfully expansive, infinite heart of Chaitanya; one who would see in every sect the same spirit working, the same God; one who would see God in every being, one whose heart would weep for the poor, for the weak, for the outcast, for the downtrodden, for every one in this world, inside India or outside India; and at the same time whose grand brilliant intellect would conceive of such noble thoughts as would harmonise all conflicting sects, not only in India but outside of India, and bring a marvellous harmony, the universal religion of head and heart into existence. Such a man was born, and I had the good fortune to sit at his feet for years. Let me now only mention the great Sri Ramakrishna, the fulfilment of the Indian sages, the sage for the time, one whose teaching is just now, in the present time, most beneficial. And mark the divine power working behind the man. The son of a poor priest, born in an out-of-the-way village, unknown and unthought of, today is worshipped literally by thousands in Europe and America, and tomorrow will be worshipped by thousands more. Who knows the plans of the Lord! (III. 267-68)

From the date that the Ramakrishna Incarnation was born, has sprung the Satya-Yuga (Golden Age). In this Incarnation atheistic ideas will be destroyed by the sword of Jnana (knowledge), and the whole world will be unified by means of Bhakti (devotion) and Prema (divine love). Moreover, in this incarnation, Rajas, or the desire for name and fame, etc. is altogether absent.... There is no chance for the welfare of the world unless the condition of women is improved. It is not possible for a bird to fly on only one wing. Hence, in the Ramakrishna Incarnation, the acceptance of a woman as the Guru, hence too His preaching the motherhood of women as representations of the Divine Mother. (VI. 327-28)

Was Sri Ramakrishna the Saviour of India merely? It is this narrow idea that has brought about India's ruin, and her welfare is an impossibility so long as this is not rooted out.... The distinction between man and woman, between the rich and the poor, the literate and illiterate, Brahmins and Chandalas—he lived to root out all. And he was the harbinger of Peace—the separation between Hindus and Mohammedans, between Hindus and Christians, all are now things of the past. That fight about distinctions that there was, belonged to another era. In this Satya-Yuga the tidal wave of Sri Ramakrishna's Love has unified all. (VI. 331-35)

You see, I love our Mohammedans! It must have

been the training under Ramakrishna Paramahamsa.
We all went by his path to some extent. Of course
it was not so difficult for us as he made it for himself.
He would eat and dress like the people he wanted
to understand, take their initiation, and use their
language. 'One must learn,' he said, 'to put oneself
into another man's very soul.' And this method was
his own! No one ever before in India became
Christian and Mohammedan and Vaishnava by
turns! (*The Master as I saw Him*, pp. 228-29)

My dear brother, that Ramakrishna Paramahamsa was God incarnate, I have not the least
doubt....Without studying Ramakrishna Paramahamsa first, one can never understand the real
import of the Vedas, the Vedanta, of the *Bhagavata*
and the other Puranas. His life is a searchlight of
infinite power thrown upon the whole mass of
Indian religious thought. He was the living com-
mentary to the Vedas and to their aim. He had
lived in one life the whole cycle of the national
religious existence in India.

Whether Bhagavan Sri Krishna was born at all
we are not sure; and Avataras like Buddha and
Chaitanya are monotonous. Ramakrishna Paramahamsa is the latest and the most perfect—the concentrated embodiment of knowledge, love, renunciation, catholicity, and the desire to serve mankind.
So where is anyone to compare with him? He must
have been born in vain who cannot appreciate him!
My supreme good fortune is that I am his servant

through life after life. A single word of his to me is far
weightier than the Vedas and the Vedanta. Oh, I
am the servant of the servants of his servants, But
narrow bigotry militates against his principles, and
this makes me cross. Rather let his name be drowned
in oblivion, and his teachings bear fruit instead!
Why, was he a slave to fame? Certain fishermen
and illiterate people called Jesus Christ a God,
but the literate people killed him. Buddha was
honoured in his lifetime by a number of merchants
and cowherds. But Ramakrishna has been worshipped in his lifetime—towards the end of this
nineteenth century—by the demons and giants of
the university as God incarnate. (VII. 481-82)

In point of character, Paramahamsa Deva beats
all previous records; and as regards teaching, he
was more liberal, more original and more progres-
sive than all his predecessors. In other words, the
older Teachers were rather one-sided, while the
teaching of this new Incarnation or Teacher is
that the best point of yoga, devotion, knowledge
and work must be combined now so as to form a
new society.... The older ones were no doubt good,
but this is the new religion of this age—the synthesis
of yoga, knowledge, devotion and work. (VII.
493)

Now the great conclusion is that Ramakrishna
has no peer; nowhere else in this world exists that
unprecedented perfection, that wonderful kindness

for all that does not stop to justify itself, that intense
sympathy for man in bondage. Either he must be
the Avatara as he himself used to say, or else the
ever-perfected divine man, whom the Vedanta
speaks of as the free one, who assumes a body for
the good of humanity. This is my conviction sure
and certain; and the worship of such a divine man
has been referred to by Patanjali in the aphorism:
'Or the goal may be attained by meditating on a
Saint.' (VI. 231-32)

Prophets preach, but the Incarnations like Jesus,
Buddha, Ramakrishna, can give religion; one
glance, one touch is enough. (VII. 8)

All that I am, all that the world itself will some
day be, is owing to my Master, Sri Ramakrishna,
who incarnated and experienced and taught this
wonderful unity which underlies everything, having
discovered it alike in Hinduism, in Islam, and in
Christianity. (V. 414)

It was not the words of Sri Ramakrishna but the
life he lived that was wanted, and that is yet to be
written. After all, this world is a series of pictures,
and man-making is the great interest running
through. We were all watching the making of men,
and that alone. Sri Ramakrishna was always
weeding out and rejecting the old, he always chose
the young for his disciples. (*Reminiscences of Swami
Vivekananda*, p. 280)

Sri Ramakrishna's purity was that of a baby. He never touched money in his life and lust was absolutely annihilated in him. Do not go to great religious teachers to learn physical science, their whole energy has gone to the spiritual. In Sri Ramakrishna Paramahamsa the man was all dead and only God remained; he actually could not see sin, he was literally 'of purer eyes than to behold iniquity'. The purity of these few Paramahamsas is all that holds the world together. If they should all die out and leave it, the world would go to pieces. They do good by simply being, and they know it not; they just are. (VII. 85)

Sri Ramakrishna wept and prayed to the Divine Mother to send him such a one to talk with as would not have in him the slightest tinge of Kama-Kanchana; for he would say, 'My lips burn when I talk with the worldly-minded'. He also used to say that he could not even bear the touch of the worldly-minded and the impure. The King of the Sannyasins (Sri Ramakrishna) can never be preached by men of the world. Without renunciation religion can never stand. (V. 261)

Sri Ramakrishna came to teach the religion of today, constructive, not destructive. He had to go afresh to Nature to ask for facts and he got scientific religion, which never says 'believe', but 'see'; 'I see, and you too can see'. Use the same means and you will reach the same vision. God will come to

everyone, harmony is within the reach of all. Sri
Ramakrishna's teachings are 'the gist of Hinduism';
they were not peculiar to him. Nor did he claim
that they were: he cared naught for name or fame.
(VII. 24)

Ramakrishna Paramahamsa was the only man
who ever had the courage to say that we must
speak to all men in their own language! (VIII. 263)

He [Ramakrishna] knew nothing of Vedanta,
nothing of theories! He was contented to live that
great life and to leave it to others to explain.
(*The Master as I Saw Him*, p. 36)

When my Master, Sri Ramakrishna, fell ill, a
Brahmin suggested to him that he apply his tremendous mental power to cure himself; he said that if
my Master would only concentrate his mind on the
diseased part of the body, it would heal. Sri Ramakrishna answered, 'What! Bring down the mind
that I've given to God to this little body!' He
refused to think of body and illness. His mind was
continually conscious of God; it was dedicated to
Him utterly. He would not use it for any other
purpose. (VIII. 110-11)

We cannot say how much a man can grow in
one life. You have no reason to say that this much
a man can do and no more. Circumstances can
hasten him wonderfully. Can there be any limit

then, till you come to perfection?...Yogis say, that all great Incarnations and Prophets are such men; that they reached perfection in this one life. We have had such men at all periods of the world's history and at all times. Quite recently, there was such a man who lived the life of the whole human race and reached the end—even in this life. (II. 18-19)

In the Ramakrishna Incarnation there is knowledge, devotion, and love—infinite knowledge, infinite love, infinite work, infinite compassion for all beings. (VI. 320)

Jnana is all right; but there is the danger of its becoming dry intellectualism. Love is great and noble; but it may die away in meaningless sentimentalism.

A harmony of all these is the thing required. Ramakrishna was such a harmony. Such beings are few and far between; but keeping him and his teachings as the ideal, we can move on.

God, though everywhere, can be known to us in and through human character. No character was ever so perfect as Ramakrishna's, and that should be the centre round which we ought to rally, at the same time allowing everybody to regard him in his own light, either as God, Saviour, teacher, model, or great man, just as he pleases. (IV. 356)

'Ramakrishna is worshipped by thousands today,

Professor (Max Müller),' I said. 'To whom else shall worship be accorded, if not to such,' was the answer.

Max Müller is a Vedantist of Vedantists. He has, indeed, caught the real soul of the melody of the Vedanta, in the midst of all its settings of harmonies and discords—the one light that lightens the sects and creeds of the world, the Vedanta, the one principle of which all religions are only applications. And what was Ramakrishna Paramahamsa? The practical demonstration of this ancient principle, the embodiment of India that is past, and a foreshadowing of the India that is to be, the bearer of spiritual light unto nations. (IV. 280-81)

Such a synthesis of universal ideas you will not find in the history of the world again. Understand from this who was born in the person of Sri Ramakrishna.... You will see only a little manifestation of what has been done. In time the whole world must accept the universal and catholic ideas of Sri Ramakrishna and of this, only the beginning has been made. Before this flood everybody will be swept off. He himself is his own parallel. Has he any exemplar? (VII. 262-64)

The more advanced a society or nation is in spirituality, the more is that society or nation civilized. No nation can be said to have become civilized only because it has succeeded in increasing the comforts of material life by bringing into use

lots of machinery and things of that sort. The
present day civilization of the West is multiplying
day by day only the wants and distresses of men.
On the other hand, the ancient Indian civilization,
by showing people the way to spiritual advancement, doubtless succeeded, if not in removing once
for all, at least in lessening, in a great measure,
the material needs of men. In the present age, it
is to bring into coalition both these civilizations
that Bhagavan Sri Ramakrishna was born. (VI.
462-63)

To remove all corruption in religion, the Lord
has incarnated Himself on earth in the present age
in the person of Sri Ramakrishna. The universal
teachings that he offered, if spread all over the
world, will do good to humanity and the world.
Not for many a century past has India produced
so great, so wonderful, a teacher of religious synthesis. (VI. 465)

Do you know what the ruling sentiment amongst
us is?—Non-sectarianism. Our Lord was born to
point that out. He would accept all forms, but
would say withal that, looked at from the standpoint of the knowledge of Brahman, they were only
like illusory Maya.... Well, you have read my
lectures. But where have I built on Sri Ramakrishna's name? It is only the pure Upanishadic
religion that I have gone about preaching in the
world. (VI. 469-70)

Disciple: Did Sri Ramakrishna, out of his own lips, ever say that he was God, the all-perfect Brahman?

Swamiji: Yes, he did so many times. And he said this to all of us. One day while he was staying at the Cossipore garden, his body in imminent danger of falling off for ever, by the side of his bed I was saying in my mind: 'Well, now if you can declare that you are God, then only will I believe you are really God Himself.' It was only two days before he passed away. Immediately, he looked up towards me all on a sudden and said: 'He who was Rama, He who was Krishna, verily is He now Ramakrishna in this body. And that not merely from the standpoint of your Vedanta!' At this I was struck dumb....Take it from me, never did come to this earth such an all-perfect man as Sri Ramakrishna! In the utter darkness of the world this great man is like the shining pillar of illumination in this age! And by his light alone will man now cross the ocean of Samsara! (VI. 480)

Disciple: I have heard that Bhagavan Sri Ramakrishna used to sing the name of God very much?

Swamiji: Quite so, but his was a different case. What comparison can there be between him and ordinary men? He practised in his life all the different ideals of religion to show that each of them leads but to the One Truth. Shall you or I ever be able to do all that he has done? None of us has understood him fully. So, I do not venture to speak about him anywhere and everywhere. He only knows what he himself really was; his frame was a human one only, but everything else about him was entirely different from others.

Disciple: Do you, may I ask, believe him to be an Avatara?

Swamiji: Tell me first—what do you mean by an Avatara?

Disciple: Why, I mean one like Sri Ramachandra, Sri Krishna, Sri Gauranga, Buddha, Jesus, and others.

Swamiji: I know Bhagavan Sri Ramakrishna to be even greater than those you have just named. What to speak of believing, which is a petty thing—I *know*!

Disciple: Why do you not preach Sri Ramakrishna as an Avatara? You have, indeed, power, eloquence, and everything else needed to do it.

Swamiji: Truly, I tell you, I have understood him very little. He appears to me to have been so great that, whenever I have to speak anything of him, I am afraid lest I ignore or explain away the truth, lest my little power does not suffice, lest in trying to extol him I present his picture by painting him according to my lights and belittle him thereby! (V. 389-90)

Sri Ramakrishna is a force. You should not think that his doctrine is this or that. But he is a power, living even now in his disciples and working in the world. I saw him growing in his ideas. He is still growing. Sri Ramakrishna was both a Jivanmukta and an Acharya. (V. 269)

If you still entertain any doubt as to Sri Ramakrishna's being a jewel-expert, what then is the difference between you and a madman! Behold, hundreds of men and women of this country (America) are beginning to worship our Lord as the greatest of all Avataras! (VI. 323)

*   *   *

HIS MESSAGE

[Once Swami Vivekananda remarked: 'All the ideas that I preach are only an attempt to echo his (Ramakrishna's) ideas.' Here some teachings of Ramakrishna have been reproduced from the works of Swamiji.]

This is the message of Sri Ramakrishna to the modern world: 'Do not care for doctrines, do not care for dogmas, or sects, or churches, or temples; they count for little compared with the essence of existence in each man, which is spirituality; and the more this is developed in a man, the more powerful is he for good. Earn that first, acquire that, and criticize no one, for all doctrines and creeds have some good in them. Show by your lives that religion does not mean words, or names, or sects, but that it means spiritual realization. Only those can understand who have felt. Only those who have attained to spirituality can communicate it to others, can be great teachers of mankind. They alone are the powers of light.' (IV. 187)

My Master's message to mankind is: 'Be spiritual and realize truth for yourself.' He would have you give up for the sake of your fellow-beings. He would have you cease talking about love for your brother, and set to work to prove your words. The time has come for renunciation, for realization; and then you will see the harmony in all the religions of the world. You will know that there is no need of any quarrel. And then only will you be ready to help humanity. To proclaim and make clear the fundamental unity underlying all religions was the mission of my Master. Other teachers have taught special religions which bear their names, but this great teacher of the nineteenth century made no claim for himself. He left every religion undisturbed because he had realized that, in reality, they are all part and parcel of the one eternal religion. (IV. 187)

A great sage [Ramakrishna] used to say: 'Suppose there is a thief in a room, and somehow he comes to know that there is a vast mass of gold in the next room, and that there is only a thin partition between the rooms. What would be the condition of that thief? He would be sleepless, he would not be able to eat or do anything. His whole mind would be on getting that gold. Do you mean to say that, if all these people really believed that the Mine of Happiness, of Blessedness, of Glory were here, they would act as they do in the world, without trying to get God?' (II. 46)

Eka-Nishtha or devotion to one ideal is absolutely necessary for the beginner in the practice of religious devotion.... The growing plant must be hedged round to protect it until it has grown into a tree. The tender plant of spirituality will die, if exposed too early to the action of a constant change of ideas and ideals.... Bhagavan Ramakrishna says: 'The pearl-oyster leaves its bed at the bottom of the sea, and comes up to the surface to catch the rain-water when the star Svati is in the ascendant. It floats about on the surface of the sea with its shell wide open, until it has succeeded in catching a drop of the rain-water, and then it dives deep down to its sea-bed, and there rests until it has succeeded in fashioning a beautiful pearl out of that rain-drop.' This is indeed the most poetical and forcible way in which the theory of Ishta-Nishtha has ever been put. (III. 64, 63)

Bhagavan Ramakrishna used to tell a story of some men who went into a mango orchard and busied themselves in counting the leaves, the twigs, and the branches examining their colour, comparing their size, and noting down everything most carefully, and then got up a learned discussion on each of these topics, which were undoubtedly

3

highly interesting to them. But one of them, more
sensible than the others, did not care for all these
things, and instead thereof, began to eat the mango
fruit. And was he not wise? So leave this counting
of leaves and twigs and note-taking to others.
This kind of work has its proper place, but not here
in the spiritual domain. You never see a strong
spiritual man among these 'leaf-counters'. (III.
49-50)

I know one [Ramakrishna] whom the world used
to call mad, and this was his [Ramakrishna's]
answer: 'My friends, the whole world is a lunatic
asylum. Some are mad after worldly love, some
after name, some after fame, some after money,
some after salvation and going to heaven. In this
big lunatic asylum I am also mad, I am mad after
God. If you are mad after money, I am mad after
God. You are mad; so am I. I think my madness is
after all the best.' (III. 99-100)

His [Ramakrishna's] principle was; first form
character, first earn spirituality, and results will
come of themselves. His favourite illustration was:
'When the lotus opens, the bees come of their own
accord to seek the honey; so let the lotus of your
character be full-blown, and the results will follow.'
This is a great lesson to learn. (IV. 177)

Sri Ramakrishna used to say: 'The breeze of
mercy is already blowing, do you only hoist the

sail.' Can anybody, my boy, thrust realization upon another? One's destiny is in one's own hands—the Guru only makes this much understood. Through the power of the seed itself the tree grows, the air and water are only aids. (VI. 456)

All observances have their utility, relatively to the varying qualifications in men. It is just as Sri Ramakrishna used to say, that the mother cooks *polao* and *kalia* (rich dishes) for one son, and sago for another. (VI. 468)

As long as the idea of 'I' remains, it [relative experience] is true. And the instant the realization of 'I' as the Atman comes, this world of relative existence becomes false. What people speak of as sin is the result of weakness—is but another form of the egoistic idea —'I am the body'. When the mind gets steadfast in the truth, 'I am the Self', then you go beyond merit and demerit, virtue and vice. Sri Ramakrishna used to say: 'When the "I" dies, all trouble is at an end.' (VI. 474)

Sri Ramakrishna used to say that if you repeatedly tell a bad man that he is good, he turns in time to be good; similarly, a good man becomes bad if he is incessantly called so. (V. 357)

'When a huge tidal wave comes,' says Bhagavan Sri Ramakrishna, 'all the little brooks and ditches become full to the brim without any effort or consciousness on their own part; so when an Incarnation comes, a tidal wave of spirituality breaks upon the world, and people feel spirituality almost full in the air.' (III. 56)

The knower of Brahman never seeks his own happiness. But what is there to prevent him from doing work for the welfare of others? Whatever work he does without attachment for its fruits brings only good to the world—it is all 'for the good of many, for the happiness of the many'. Sri Ramakrishna used to say: 'They never take a false step.' (VII. 180)

Sri Ramakrishna used to say: 'In the morning and evening the mind remains highly imbued with Sattva ideas; those are the times when one should meditate with earnestness.' (VII. 248)

My Master used to say: 'God is the philosopher's stone that turns us to gold in an instant; the form remains, but the nature is changed—the human form remains, but no more can we hurt or sin.' (VII. 8)

He [Ramakrishna] said: 'That is a glorious thing that there should be so many paths, because if there were only one path, perhaps it would suit only an individual man. The more the number of paths, the more the chance for every one of us to know the truth. If I cannot be taught in one language, I will try another, and so on.' Thus his benediction was for every religion. Now, all the ideas that I preach are only an attempt to echo his ideas. (VIII. 79)

Sri Ramakrishna said: 'After the butter is churned, it can be put in water or milk and will never mix with either; so when man has once realized the Self, he can no more be contaminated by the world.' (VIII. 15)

If one man is made, it equals the result of a hundred thousand lectures. Making the mind and the lips at one, the ideas have to be practised in life. This is what Sri Ramakrishna meant by 'allowing no theft in the chamber of thought'. (VII. 135)

Sri Ramakrishna used to deprecate lukewarmness in spiritual attainments as, for instance, saying that religion would come gradually, and that there was no hurry for it. When one is thirsty, can one sit idle? Does he not run about for water? Because your thirst for spirituality has not come, therefore you are sitting idly. The desire for knowledge has not grown strong, therefore you are satisfied with the little pleasures of family life. (VII. 194)

A sage [Ramakrishna] once told me: 'To kill others one must be equipped with swords and shields, but to commit suicide a needle is sufficient;

so to teach others, much intellect and learning are necessary, but not so for your own self-illumination.' (I. 413)

The master said, 'My child, if you desire after God, God shall come to you.' The disciple did not understand his master fully. One day both went to bathe in a river, and the master said, 'Plunge in', and the boy did so. In a moment the master was upon him, holding him down. He would not let the boy come up. When the boy struggled and was exhausted, he let him go. 'Yes, my child, how did you feel there?' 'Oh, the desire for a breath of air!' 'Do you have that kind of desire for God?' 'No, sir.' 'Have that kind of desire for God, and you shall have God.' (V. 251)

My Master used to say, 'All is God; but tiger-God is to be shunned. All water is water; but we avoid dirty water for drinking.' (VII. 13)

Six blind men lived in a village. They could not see the elephant, but they went out and felt [of] him. One put his hand on the elephant's tail, one of them on his side, one on his trunk, one on his ear. They began to describe the elephant. One said he was like a rope; one said he was like a great wall; one said he was like a boa constrictor, and another said he was like a fan. They finally came to blows and went to pummelling each other. A man who could see came along and inquired the trouble, and the blind men said they had seen the elephant and disagreed because one accused the other of lying. 'Well,' said the man, 'you have all lied; you are blind, and neither of you have seen it.' That is what is the matter with our religion. We let the blind see the elephant. (VII. 420)

Thought is all important, for 'what we think we become'. There was once a Sannyasin, a holy man, who sat under a tree and taught the people. He drank milk and ate only fruit, and made endless 'Pranayamas', and felt himself to be very holy. In the same village lived an evil woman. Every day the Sannyasin went and warned her that her wickedness would lead her to hell. The poor woman, unable to change her method of life which was her only means of livelihood, was still much moved by the terrible future depicted by the Sannyasin. She wept and prayed to the Lord, begging Him to forgive her because she could not help herself. By and by both the holy man and the evil woman died. The angels came and bore her to heaven while the demons claimed the soul of the Sannyasin. 'Why is this!' he exclaimed, 'have I not lived a most holy life, and preached holiness to everybody? Why should I be taken to hell while this wicked woman is taken to heaven?' 'Because,' answered the demons, 'while she was forced to commit unholy acts, her mind was always fixed on the Lord and she sought deliverance, which has now come to her. But you, on the contrary, while you perfomed only holy acts, had your mind always fixed on the wickedness of others. You saw only sin and thought only of sin, so now you have to go to that place where only sin is.' (VIII. 19-20)

Some poor fishwives, overtaken by a violent storm, found refuge in the garden of a rich man. He received them kindly, fed them, and left them to rest in a summer-house, surrounded by exquisite flowers which filled all the air with their rich perfume. The women lay down in this sweet-smelling paradise, but could not sleep. They missed something out of their lives and could not be happy without it. At last one of the women arose and went to the place where they had left their fish baskets, brought them to the summer-house and then once more happy in the familiar smell, they were all soon sound asleep. Let not the world be our 'fish basket' which we have to depend upon for enjoyment. (VIII. 29)

Those who are pure always in body, mind, and speech, who have strong devotion, who discriminate between the real and the unreal, who persevere in meditation and contemplation—upon them alone the grace of the Lord descends. The Lord, however, is beyond all natural laws—is not under any rules and regulations, or, just as Sri Ramakrishna used to say, He has the child's nature—and that's why we find some failing to get any response even after calling on Him for millions of births, while some one else whom we regard as a sinful or penitent man, or a disbeliever, would have Illumination in a flash! On the latter the Lord perhaps lavishes His grace quite unsolicited! You may argue that this man had good merits stored up from previous life, but the mystery is really difficult to understand. Sri Ramakrishna used to say sometimes, 'Do rely on Him; be like the dry leaf at the mercy of the wind'; and again he would say, 'The wind of His grace is always blowing, what you need to do is to unfurl your sail'. (VI. 481-82)

This body is made up of two sorts of Karma consisting of virtue and vice—injurious vice and non-injurious virtue. A thorn is pricking my body, and I take another thorn to take it out and then throw both away. A man desiring to be perfect takes a thorn of virtue and with it takes off the thorn of vice. (VI. 111)

*   *   *

THE SIGNIFICANCE OF HIS LIFE AND TEACHINGS

In a narrow society there is depth and intensity of spirituality. The narrow stream is very rapid. In a catholic society, along with the breadth of vision we find a proportionate loss in depth and intensity. But the life of Sri Ramakrishna upsets all records of history. It is a remarkable phenomenon that in Sri Ramakrishna there has been an assemblage of ideas deeper than the sea and vaster than the skies.

We must interpret the Vedas in the light of the experience of Sri Ramakrishna. Shankaracharya and all other commentators made the tremendous mistake to think that the whole of the Vedas spoke the same truth. Therefore they were guilty of torturing those of the apparently conflicting Vedic texts which go against their own doctrines, into the meaning of their particular schools. As, in the olden times, it was the Lord alone, the deliverer of the *Gita*, who partially harmonized these apparently conflicting statements, so, with a view to completely settling this dispute, immensely magnified in the process of time, He Himself has come as Sri Ramakrishna. Therefore no one can truly understand the Vedas and Vedanta, unless one studies them in the light of the utterances of Sri Ramakrishna who first exemplified in his life and taught that these scriptural statements which appear to the cursory view as contradictory, are meant for different grades of aspirants and are arranged in the order of evolution. The whole world will undoubtedly forget its fights and disputes and be united in a fraternal tie in religious and other matters as a consequence of these teachings.

If there is anything which Sri Ramakrishna has urged us to give up as carefully as lust and wealth, it is the limiting of the infinitude of God by circumscribing it within narrow bounds. Whoever, therefore, will try to limit the infinite ideals of Sri Ramakrishna in that way, will go against him and be his enemy.

One of his own utterances is that those who have seen the chameleon only once, know only one colour of the animal, but those who have lived under the tree, know all the colours that it puts on. For this reason, no saying of Sri Ramakrishna can be accepted as authentic, unless it is verified by those who constantly lived with him and whom he brought up to fulfil his life's mission.

Such a unique personality, such a synthesis of the utmost of Jnana, Yoga, Bhakti and Karma, has never before appeared among mankind. The life of Sri Ramakrishna proves that the greatest breadth, the highest catholicity and the utmost intensity can exist side by side in the same individual, and that society also can be constructed like that, for society is nothing but an aggregate of individuals.

He is the true disciple and follower of Sri Ramakrishna, whose character is perfect and all-sided like this. The formation of such a perfect character is the ideal of this age, and everyone should strive for that alone. (*Prabuddha Bharata*, March 1929)

RAMAKRISHNA: THE NATIONAL IDEAL

Brothers, you have touched another chord in my heart, the deepest of all, and that is the mention of my teacher, my master, my hero, my ideal, my God in life—Sri Ramakrishna Paramahamsa. If there has been anything achieved by me, by thoughts, or words, or deeds, if from my lips has ever fallen one word that has helped any one in the world, I lay no claim to it, it was his. But if there have been curses falling from my lips, if there has been hatred coming out of me, it is all mine and not his. All that has been weak has been mine, and all that has been life-giving, strengthening, pure, and holy, has been his inspiration, his words and he himself. Yes, my friends, the world has yet to know that man. We read in the history of the world about prophets and their lives, and these come down to us through centuries of writings and workings by their disciples. Through thousands of years of chiselling and modelling, the lives of the great prophets of yore come down to us; and yet, in my opinion, not one stands so high in brilliance as that life which I saw with my own eyes, under whose shadow I have lived, at whose feet I have learnt everything—the life of Ramakrishna Paramahamsa.

Ay, this boy born of poor Brahmin parents in an out-of-the-way village of which very few of you have even heard, is literally being worshipped in lands which have been fulminating against heathen worship for centuries. Whose power is it? Is it mine or yours? It is none else than the power which was manifested here as Ramakrishna Paramahamsa. For, you and I and sages and prophets, nay, even Incarnations, the whole universe, are but manifestations of power more or less individualized, more or less concentrated. Here has been a manifestation of an immense power, just the very beginning of whose workings we are seeing, and before this generation passes away, you will see more wonderful workings of that power. It has come just in time for the regeneration of India, for we forget from time to time the vital power that must always work in India.

Each nation has its own peculiar method of work. Some work through politics, some through social reforms, some through other lines. With us, religion is the only ground along which we can move. The Englishman can understand even religion through politics. Perhaps the American can understand even religion through social reforms. But the Hindu can understand even politics when it is given through religion; sociology must come through religion, everything must come through religion. For that is the theme, the rest are the variations in the national life-music. And that was in danger. It seemed that we were going to change this theme in our national life, that we were going to exchange the backbone of our existence, as it were, that we were trying to replace a spiritual by

a political backbone. And if we could have succeeded, the result would have been annihilation.
But it was not to be. So this power became manifest.
I do not care in what light you understand this
great sage, it matters not how much respect you
pay to him, but I challenge you face to face with
the fact that here is a manifestation of the most
marvellous power that has been for several centuries
in India and it is your duty, as Hindus, to study this
power, to find what has been done for the regeneration, for the good of India, and for the good of the
whole human race through it. Ay, long before ideas
of universal religion and brotherly feeling between
different sects were mooted and discussed in any
country in the world, here, in sight of this city, had
been living a man whose whole life was a Parlia-
ment of Religions as it should be.

The highest ideal in our scriptures is the impersonal, and would to God everyone of us here were
high enough to realize that impersonal ideal; but,
as that cannot be, it is absolutely necessary for the
vast majority of human beings to have a personal
ideal; and no nation can rise, can become great,
can work at all, without enthusiastically coming
under the banner of one of these great ideals in
life. Political ideals, personages representing political
ideals, even social ideals, commercial ideals, would
have no power in India. We want spiritual ideals
before us, we want enthusiastically to gather round
grand spiritual names. Our heroes must be spiritual.
Such a hero has been given to us in the person of

Ramakrishna Paramahamsa. If this nation wants to rise, take my word for it, it will have to rally enthusiastically round this name. It does not matter who preaches Ramakrishna Paramahamsa, whether I, or you, or anybody else. But him I place before you, and it is for you to judge, and for the good of our race, for the good of our nation, to judge now, what you shall do with this great ideal of life. One thing we are to remember, that it was the purest of all lives that you have ever seen, or let me tell you distinctly, that you have ever read of. And before you is the fact that it is the most marvellous manifestation of soul-power that you can read of, much less expect to see. Within ten years of his passing away, this power has encircled the globe; that fact is before you. In duty bound, therefore, for the good of our race, for the good of our religion, I place this great spiritual ideal before you. Judge him not through me. I am only a weak instrument. Let not his character be judged by seeing me. It was so great that if I or any other of his disciples spent hundreds of lives, we could not do justice to a millionth part of what he really was. Judge for yourselves; in the heart of your hearts is the Eternal Witness, and may He, the same Ramakrishna Paramahamsa, for the good of our nation, for the welfare of our country, and for the good of humanity, open your hearts, make you true and steady to work for the immense change which must come, whether we exert ourselves or not. For the work of the Lord does not wait for the like of you or me. He can raise

His workers from the dust by hundreds and by thousands. It is a glory and a privilege that we are allowed to work at all under Him. (III. 312-16)

Ever since the advent of Sri Ramakrishna the eastern horizon has been aglow with the dawning rays of the sun which in course of time will illumine the country with the splendour of the midday sun. (VII. 183)

In order that a nation may rise, it must have a high ideal. Now, that ideal is, of course, the abstract Brahman. But as you all cannot be inspired by an abstract ideal, you must have a personal ideal. You have got that in the person of Sri Ramakrishna. The reason why other personages cannot be our ideal now is, that their days are gone; and in order that Vedanta may come to everyone, there must be a person who is in sympathy with the present generation. This is fulfilled in Sri Ramakrishna. So now you should place him before everyone. Whether one accepts him as a Sadhu or an Avatara, does not matter. (VII. 413)

It has become a trite saying that idolatry is wrong, and every man swallows it at the present time without questioning. I once thought so, and to pay the penalty of that I had to learn my lesson sitting at the feet of a man who realized everything through idols; I allude to Ramakrishna Parama-hamsa. If such Ramakrishna Paramahamsas are

produced by idol-worship, what will you have—
the reformer's creed or any number of idols? I
want an answer. Take a thousand idols more if you
can produce Ramakrishna Paramahamsas through
idol-worship, and may God speed you! (III. 218)

Don't you know how an illiterate boy, possessed
of renunciation, turned the heads of your great old
Pandits? Once at the Dakshineswar Temple the
Brahmana who was in charge of the worship of
Vishnu broke a leg of the image. Pandits were
brought together at a meeting to give their opinions,
and they, after consulting old books and man-
uscripts, declared that the worship of this broken
image could not be sanctioned according to the
Shastras and a new image would have to be con-
secrated. There was, consequently, a great stir.
Sri Ramakrishna was called at last. He heard and
asked, 'Does a wife forsake her husband in case he
becomes lame?' What followed? The Pandits were
struck dumb, all their Shastric commentaries and
erudition could not withstand the force of this
simple statement. If what you say was true, why
should Sri Ramakrishna come down to this earth,
and why should he discourage mere book-learning
so much? That new life-force which he brought with
him has to be instilled into learning and education,
and then the real work will be done. (V. 870)

The artistic faculty was highly developed in our
Lord, Sri Ramakrishna, and he used to say that

4

without this faculty none can be truly spiritual.... It is my opinion that Sri Ramakrishna was born to vivify all branches of art and culture in this country. (V. 259, VII. 205)

Simplicity is the secret. My ideal of language is my Master's language, most colloquial and yet most expressive. It must express the thought which is intended to be conveyed. (V. 259)

When my Master left the body, we were a dozen penniless and unknown young men. Against us were a hundred powerful organizations, struggling hard to nip us in the bud. But Sri Ramakrishna had given us one great gift, the desire, and the lifelong struggle not to talk alone, but *live the life*. And today all India knows and reverences the Master, and the truths he taught are spreading like wild fire. (VIII. 348)

Sri Ramakrishna is our centre. Each one of us is a ray of that light centre.... India is already Ramakrishna's whether I live a few years more or not. (VII. 170, 501)

My hope is to see again the strong points of that India, reinforced by the strong points of this age, only in a natural way. The new stage of things must be a *growth* from within....

But you may ask—what is the place of Rama- krishna in this scheme?

He is the method, that wonderful unconscious method! He did not understand himself. He knew nothing of England or the English, save that they were queer folk from over the sea. But he lived that great life; and I read the meaning. Never a word of condemnation for any! Once I had been attacking one of our sects of diabolists. I had been raving on for three hours, and he had listened quietly. 'Well, well!' said the old man as I finished, 'perhaps every house may have back door. Who knows?' (VIII. 266-67)

Question: What part will the Ramakrishna Mission take in the regenerating work of India?

Swamiji: From this Math will go out men of character who will deluge the world with spirituality. This will be followed by revivals in other lines. Thus Brahmins, Kshatriyas, and Vaishyas will be produced. The Shudra caste will exist no longer —their work being done by machinery. The present want of India is the Kshatriya force. (V. 316)

Sri Ramakrishna was a wonderful gardener. Therefore he has made a bouquet of different flowers and formed his Order. All different types and ideas have come into it and many more will come. Sri Ramakrishna used to say: 'Whoever has prayed to God sincerely for one day, must come here.' (VII. 258)

India can only rise by sitting at the feet of Sri

Ramakrishna. His life and his teachings are to be spread far and wide, are to be made to penetrate every pore of Hindu society. Who will do it? Who are to take up the flag of Ramakrishna and march for the salvation of the world? Who are to stem the tide of degeneration at the sacrifice of name and fame, wealth and enjoyment—nay of every hope of this or other worlds? A few young men have jumped in the breach, have sacrificed themselves. They are a few; we want a few thousands of such as they and *they will come*. I am glad that our Lord has put it in your mind to be one of them. Glory unto him on whom falls the Lord's choice. (VI. 281)

He alone is a child of Sri Ramakrishna who is moved to pity for all creatures and exerts himself for them even at the risk of incurring personal damnation, 'others are vulgar people'. Whoever, at this great spiritual juncture, will stand up with a courageous heart and go on spreading from door to door, from village to village, his message, is alone my brother, and a son of His. This is the test, he who is Ramakrishna's child does not seek his personal good. 'They wish to do good to others even when at the point of death.' Those that care for their personal comforts and seek a lazy life, who are ready to sacrifice all before their personal whims, are none of us; let them pack off, while yet there is time. Propagate his character, his teachings, his religion. This is the only spiritual practice, the only

worship, this verily is the means, and this the goal.
Arise! Arise! A huge spiritual tidal wave is coming!
Onward! Onward! (VI. 294)

HINDUISM AND SRI RAMAKRISHNA

By the word 'Shastras' the Vedas without beginning or end are meant. In matters of religious duty the Vedas are the only capable authority.

The Puranas and other religious scriptures are all denoted by the word 'Smriti'. And their authority goes so far as they follow the Vedas and do not contradict them.

Truth is of two kinds: (1) that which is cognizable by the five ordinary senses of man, and by reasonings based thereon; (2) that which is cognizable by the subtle, supersensuous power of Yoga.

Knowledge acquired by the first means is called science; and knowledge acquired by the second is called the Vedas.

The whole body of supersensuous truths, having no beginning or end, and called by the name of the Vedas, is ever-existent. The Creator Himself is creating, preserving, and destroying the universe with the help of these truths.

The person in whom this supersensuous power is manifested is called a Rishi, and the supersensuous truths which he realizes by this power are called the Vedas.

This Rishihood, this power of supersensuous perception of the Vedas, is real religion. And so long as this does not develop in the life of an initiate, so long is religion a mere empty word to him, and it is to be understood that he has not taken yet the first step in religion.

The authority of the Vedas extends to all ages, climes and persons; that is to say, their application is not confined to any particular place, time, and persons.

The Vedas are the only exponent of the universal religion.

Although the supersensuous vision of truths is to be met with in some measure in our Puranas and Itihasas and in the religious scriptures of other races, still the fourfold scripture known among the Aryan race as the Vedas being the first, the most complete, and the most undistorted collection of spiritual truths, deserve to occupy the highest place among all scriptures, command the respect of all nations of the earth, and furnish the rationale of all their respective scriptures.

With regard to the whole Vedic collection of truths discovered by the Aryan race, this also has to be understood that those portions alone which do not refer to purely secular matters and which do not merely record tradition or history, or merely provide incentives to duty, form the Vedas in the real sense.

The Vedas are divided into two portions, the Jnana-kanda (knowledge-portion) and the Karma-kanda (ritual-portion). The ceremonies and the fruits of the Karma-kanda are confined within the limits of the world of Maya, and therefore they have been undergoing and will undergo transformation according to the law of change which operates through time, space, and personality.

Social laws and customs likewise, being based on this Karma-kanda, have been changing and will continue to change hereafter. Minor social usages also will be recognized and accepted when they are compatible with the spirit of the true scriptures and the conduct and example of holy sages. But blind allegiance only to usages such as are repugnant to the spirit of the Shastras and the conduct of holy sages has been one of the main causes of the downfall of the Aryan race.

It is the Jnana-kanda or the Vedanta only that has for all time commanded recognition for leading men across Maya and bestowing salvation on them through the practice of Yoga, Bhakti, Jnana, or selfless work; and as its validity and authority remain unaffected by any limitations of time, place or persons, it is the only exponent of the universal and eternal religion for all mankind.

The Samhitas of Manu and other sages, following the lines laid down in the Karma-kanda, have mainly ordained rules of conduct conducive to social welfare, according to the exigencies of time, place, and persons. The Puranas etc. have taken up the truths embedded in the Vedanta and have explained them in detail in the course of describing the exalted life and deeds of Avataras and others. They have each emphasized, besides, some out of the infinite aspects of the Divine Lord to teach men about them.

But when by the process of time, fallen from the true ideals and rules of conduct and devoid of the spirit of renunciation, addicted only to blind usages, and degraded in intellect, the descendants of the Aryans failed to appreciate even the spirit of these Puranas etc. which taught men of ordinary intelligence the abstruse truths of the Vedanta in concrete form and diffuse language and appeared antagonistic to one another on the surface, because of each inculcating with special emphasis only particular aspects of the spiritual ideal—

And when, as a consequence, they reduced India, the fair land of religion, to a scene of almost infernal confusion by breaking up piecemeal the one Eternal Religion of the Vedas (Sanatana Dharma), the grand synthesis of all the aspects of the spiritual ideal, into conflicting sects and by seeking to sacrifice one another in the flames of sectarian hatred and intolerance—

Then it was that Sri Bhagavan Ramakrishna incarnated himself in India, to demonstrate what the true religion of the Aryan race is; to show where amidst all its many divisions and offshoots, scattered over the land in the course of its immemorial history, lies the true unity of the Hindu religion, which by its overwhelming number of sects discordant to superficial view, quarrelling constantly with each other and abounding in customs divergent in every way, has constituted itself a misleading enigma for our countrymen and the butt of contempt for foreigners; and above all, to hold up before men,

for their lasting welfare, as a living embodiment of
the Sanatana Dharma, his own wonderful life into
which he infured the universal spirit and character
of this Dharma, so long cast into oblivion by the
process of time.

In order to show how the Vedic truths—eternally
existent as the instrument with the Creator in His
work of creation, preservation, and dissolution—
reveal themselves spontaneously in the minds of the
Rishis purified from all impressions of worldly
attachment, and because such verification and
confirmation of the scriptural truths will help the
revival, reinstatement, and spread of religion—the
Lord, though the very embodiment of the Vedas, in
this His new incarnation has thoroughly discarded
all external forms of learning.

That the Lord incarnates again and again in
human form for the protection of the Vedas or the
true religion, and of Brahminhood or the ministry
of that religion—is a doctrine well established in
the Puranas etc.

The waters of a river falling in a cataract acquire
greater velocity, the rising wave after a hollow
swells higher; so after every spell of decline, the
Aryan society recovering from all the evils by the
merciful dispensation of Providence has risen the
more glorious and powerful—such is the testimony
of history.

After rising from every fall, our revived society
is expressing more and more its innate eternal
perfection, and so also the omnipresent Lord in

each successive incarnation is manifesting Himself more and more.

Again and again has our country fallen into a swoon, as it were, and again and again has India's Lord, by the manifestation of Himself, revivified her.

But greater than the present deep dismal night, now almost over, no pall of darkness had ever before enveloped this holy land of ours. And compared with the depth of this fall, all previous falls appear like little hoof-marks.

Therefore, before the effulgence of this new awakening, the glory of all past revivals in her history will pale like stars before the rising sun; and compared with this mighty manifestation of renewed strength, all the many past epochs of such restoration will be as child's play.

The various constituent ideals of the Religion Eternal, during its present state of decline, have been lying scattered here and there for want of competent men to realize them—some being preserved partially among small sects and some completely lost.

But strong in the strength of this new spiritual renaissance, men, after reorganizing these scattered and disconnected spiritual ideals, will be able to comprehend and practise them in their own lives and also to recover from oblivion those that are lost. And as the sure pledge of this glorious future, the all-merciful Lord has manifested in the present age, as stated above, an incarnation which in point of completeness in revelation, its synthetic harmonizing of all ideals, and its promoting of every sphere of spiritual culture, surpasses the manifestations of all past ages.

So at the very dawn of this momentous epoch, the reconciliation of all aspects and ideals of religious thought and worship is being proclaimed. This boundless, all-embracing idea had been lying inherent, but so long concealed, in the Religion Eternal and its scriptures, and now rediscovered, it is being declared to humanity in a trumpet voice.

This epochal new dispensation is the harbinger of great good to the whole world, specially to India; and the inspirer of this dispensation, Sri Bhagavan Ramakrishna, is the reformed and remodelled manifestation of all the past great epoch-makers in religion. O man, have faith in this, and lay it to heart.

The dead never return; the past night does not reappear; a spent-up tidal wave does not rise anew; neither does man inhabit the same body over again. So from the worship of the dead past, O man, we invite you to the worship of the living present; from the regretful brooding over bygones, we invite you to the activities of the present; from the waste of energy in retracing lost and demolished pathways, we call you back to broad new-laid highways lying very near. He that is wise, let him understand.

Of that power, which at the very first impulse has roused distant echoes from all the four quarters of the globe, conceive in your mind the manifestation in its fullness; and discarding all idle misgivings, weaknesses, and the jealousies characteristic of enslaved peoples, come and help in the turning of this mighty wheel of the new dispensation!

With the conviction firmly rooted in your heart that you are the servants of the Lord, His children, helpers in the fulfilment of His purposes, enter the arena of work. (VI. 181-86)

* * *

He [Ramakrishna] was the embodiment of all the past religious thoughts of India. His life alone made me understand what the Shastras really meant, and the whole plan and scope of the old Shastras. (VI. 311-12)

It is a character, a life, a centre, a God-man that must lead the way, that must be the centre round which all other elements will gather themselves and then fall like a tidal wave upon the society, carrying all before it, washing away all impurities. Again, a piece of wood can only easily be cut along the grain. So the old Hinduism can only be reformed through Hinduism, and not through the new-fangled reform movements. At the same time the reformers must be able to unite in themselves the culture of both the East and the West. Now do you not think that you have already seen the nucleus of such a great movement, that you have heard the low rumblings of the coming tidal wave? That centre, that God-man to lead was born in India. He was the great Ramakrishna Paramahamsa, and round him this band is slowly gathering. They will do the work. (VIII. 308-09)

Now this seems, therefore, to be the great point of difference between the dualist and the Advaitist. You will see a regular bull-fight going on about these various sects and things.... Thus it remains. Then came one whose life was the explanation, whose life was the working out of the harmony that is the background of all the different sects of India, I mean Ramakrishna Paramahamsa. It is his life that explains that both of these are necessary, that they are like the geocentric and the heliocentric theories in astronomy. (III. 348-49)

Devotion as taught by Narada, he [Ramakrishna] used to preach to the masses, those who were incapable of any higher training. He used generally to teach dualism. As a rule, he never taught Advaitism. But he taught it to me. (VII. 412)

Question: Did Buddha teach that the many was real and the ego unreal, while orthodox Hinduism regards the One as the Real, and the many as unreal?

Swamiji: Yes. And what Ramakrishna Paramahamsa and I have added to this is that the Many and the One are the same Reality, perceived by the same mind at different times and in different attitudes. (*The Master as I Saw Him*, p. 23)

The life of Sri Ramakrishna was an extraordinary searchlight under whose illumination one is able to really understand the whole scope of Hindu religion. He was the object-lesson of all the theoretical knowledge given in the Shastras (scriptures). He showed by his life what the Rishis and Avataras really wanted to teach. The books were theories, he was the realization. This man had in fifty-one years lived the five thousand years of national spiritual life, and so raised himself to be an object-lesson for future generations. (V. 53)

Question: Your last remarks, Swamiji, raise another question. In what sense is Sri Ramakrishna a part of this awakened Hinduism?

Swamiji: That is not for me to determine. I have never preached personalities. My own life is guided by the enthusiasm of this great soul; but others will decide for themselves how far they share in this attitude. Inspiration is not filtered out to the world through one channel, however great. Each generation should be inspired afresh. (V. 227)

GLORY TO RAMAKRISHNA!

A HYMN TO THE DIVINITY OF SRI RAMAKRISHNA

[Rendered from the Bengali. It is an aratrika hymn.]

We salute Thee!
    Lord! Adored of the world,
Samsara's bondage breaker, taintless Thou,
Embodiment of blessed qualities,
Thou transcendest all Gunas; human form
Thou bearest.
    Thee we salute and adore!

Refuge of mind and speech, Thou art beyond
The reach of either. Radiance art Thou
In all radiance that is. The heart's cave
Is by Thy visitance resplendent made.
Verily Thou art that which dispelleth
The densest darkness of Tamas in man.

One glancing vision at Thine eyes divine
Cleared by the collyrium of Jnana
Defies delusion. O Thou blotter-out
Of all the taints of sin, Intelligence
Pure, unmingled, is Thy form. Of the world
Thou art embellisher. Self-luminous
Art Thou. O Ocean of feeling sublime
And of Love Divine, O God-maddened One,
Devotees win Thy blessed feet, and cross
Safely the swelling sea of Samsara.

O Lord of the world, through Thy Yoga power
Thou shinest as the Incarnation clear
Of this our time. O Thou of strict restraint,
Only through Thine unstinted grace we see
The mind in Samadhi completely merged;
Mercy Incarnate! austere are Thy deeds.

Thou dealest to the evil of Misery
Destruction. Kali's binding cords
Are cut by Thee asunder. Thine own life
Thou gavest freely, O sweet Sacrifice,
O best of men! O Saviour of the world!

Devoid wert Thou of the idea of sex,
Thought of possession charmed Thee not. To Thee
Obnoxious was all pleasure. Give to us,
O greatest among Tyagis, love intense
Unto Thy sacred feet; give, we implore!

Fearless art Thou, and past all gloom of doubt;
Thy mind is wrapt in its own firm resolve;
Thy lovers, whose devotion mounts above
The realm of reason, who renounce the pride
Of caste and parentage, of name and fame—
Their safe refuge art Thou alone, O Lord!

My one true treasure is Thy blessed feet,
Reaching which the whole universe itself
Seems like a puddle in the hollow made
By hoof of passing cow.

O offering
To Love! O seer of equality
In all! O verily, in Thee the pain
And evil of this mortal world escapes,
And vanishes, O cherished One, in Thee!

Lo! In variety of melody
Forth-breaking in fine harmony most sweet,
Hymns of Thy devotees, accompanied
By mridanga playing with music's grace,
Fill the air, in evening worship to Thee.

(IV. 504-06)

HYMNS TO SRI RAMAKRISHNA

[*These two hymns were composed by Swamiji in Sanskrit
in November 1898 at the rented Math of Belur.*]

I

1. Om! Hrim! Thou art the True, the Imperturb-
able One, transcending the three Gunas and yet
adored for Thy virtues! Inasmuch as I do not
worship day and night with yearning Thy com-
passionate lotus feet which destroy all ignorance,
therefore, O Thou friend of the lowly, Thou art my
only refuge.

2. Spiritual powers, reverence, and worship,
which put an end to this cycle of birth and death,
are enough indeed to lead to the greatest Truth.
But this while finding utterance through the mouth
is not at all being brought home to my heart.

Therefore, O Thou friend of the lowly, Thou art my only refuge.

3. If devotion is directed to Thee, O Ramakrishna, the way of Divine Truth, then with desires all fulfilled in Thee, they forthwith cross over this sea of Rajas: for Thy feet are like nectar to mortals, quelling the waves of death. Therefore, O Thou friend of the lowly, Thou art my only refuge.

4. O Thou dispeller of illusion, Thy name ending in 'shna', pure and auspicious, converts sinfulness to purity. Because, O Thou the only goal of all beings, shelter have I none, Thou art, O friend of the lowly, my only refuge.

(VIII. 172-73)

II

1. He who was Sri Rama, whose stream of love flowed with resistless might even to the Chandala (the outcaste); oh! who was ever engaged in doing good to the world though superhuman by nature, whose renown there is none to equal in the three worlds, Sita's beloved, whose body of Knowledge Supreme was covered by devotion sweet in the form of Sita.

2. He who quelled the noise, terrible like that at the time of destruction, arising from the battle [of Kurukshetra], who destroyed the terrible yet

natural night of ignorance [of Arjuna] and who roared out the *Gita* sweet and appeasing; That renowned soul is born now as Sri Ramakrishna.

3. Hail, O Lord of Men! Victory unto You! I surrender myself to my Guru, the physician for the malady of Samsara [relative existence] who is, as it were, a wave rising in the ocean of Shakti [Power], who has shown various sports of Love Divine, and who is the weapon to destroy the demon of doubt.

Hail, O Lord of Men! Victory unto You!

4. Hail, O Lord of Men! Victory unto You! I surrender myself to my Guru the Man-God, the physician for the malady of this Samsara [relative existence], whose mind ever dwelt on the non-dualistic Truth, whose personality was covered by the cloth of Supreme Devotion, who was ever active [for the good of humanity] and whose actions were all superhuman.

Hail, O Lord of Men! Victory unto You!

(VIII. 173-75)

WHOM TO FEAR?

[*These stanzas in Sanskrit form part of a letter dated 25 September 1894, addressed to the Swami's brother-disciples.*]

1. We shall crush the stars to atoms, and unhinge the universe. Don't you know who we are? We are the servants of Sri Ramakrishna.

2. It is those foolish people who identify them-selves with their bodies, that piteously cry, 'We are weak, we are low'. All this is atheism. Now that we have attained the state beyond fear, we shall have no more fear and become heroes. This indeed is theism which we, the servants of Sri Ramakrishna, will choose.

3. Giving up the attachment for the world and drinking constantly the supreme nectar of immortal-ity, for ever discarding that self-seeking spirit which is the mother of all dissension, and ever meditating on the blessed feet of our Guru which are the embodiment of all well-being, with repeated salutations we invite the whole world to participate in drinking the nectar.

4. That nectar which has been obtained by churning the infinite ocean of the Vedas, into which Brahma, Vishnu, Shiva, and the other gods have poured their strength, which is charged with the life-essence of the Avataras—Gods Incarnate on earth—Sri Ramakrishna holds that nectar in his person, in its fullest measure!

(VI. 275-76)

SALUTATIONS TO SRI RAMAKRISHNA

I

Constant salutation be to Sri Ramakrishna—the Free, the Ishvara, the Shiva-form—by whose power we and the whole world are blessed. (V. 132)

II

[Swamiji composed extempore this Sanskrit mantra for prostration before Bhagavan Sri Ramakrishna on 6 February 1898 at Ramakrishnapur, Howrah.]

I bow down to Sri Ramakrishna, who established *the* religion, embodying in himself the reality of all **religions** and being thus the foremost of divine **Incarnations.** (VI. 513)

AT THE FEET OF MY MASTER

Like a child in the wildest forest lost
I have cried and cried alone,
'Where art Thou gone, my God, my love?'
The echo answered, 'gone'.

I called on all the holy names
Of every clime and creed,
'Show me the way, in mercy, ye
Great ones who have reached the goal.'

Years then passed in bitter cry,
Each moment seemed an age,
Till one day 'midst my cries and groans
Some one seemed calling me.
A gentle soft and soothing voice
That said 'my son', 'my son'.

Again, again it seemed to speak—
The voice divine to me.
In rapture all my soul was hushed,
Entranced, enthralled in bliss.

A flash illumined all my soul;
The heart of my heart opened wide.
O joy, O bliss, what do I find!
My love, my love, you are here,
And you are here, my love, my all!

(VII. 448-49)

FIRST MEETINGS

[One day, in a literature class, Naren heard
Principal W. Hastie lecturing on Wordsworth's
The Excursion and the poet's nature-mysticism. This
led the Professor to speak of those states of deep
meditation in which outer consciousness is lost.
He told his students that such states were only
possible as the result of purity and concentration
and that they had anyway become extremely
rare in modern times. 'I have known only one
person,' he added, 'who has achieved such meditation, and that is Ramakrishna of Dakshineswar.
You will understand it better if you visit this
saint.'

According to Saradananda, in November 1881,
Naren went to the house of Surendra Nath Mitra,
who had asked him to play and sing to entertain
his guests at a party. One of these guests was
Ramakrishna.

Ramakrishna showed an eager interest in Naren
from the first moment he saw him. He called
Surendra Nath and Ram Chandra Datta and
questioned them minutely about the boy. Then,
when Naren had finished singing, Ramakrishna
spoke a few words to him, studying his face intently
as he did so. Evidently he was looking for certain
physical signs which would confirm his belief that
this was indeed one of his destined disciples. Then

he invited Naren to visit him at Dakshineswar. Naren agreed to do so.

*   *   *

When, at a later date, Ramakrishna was asked about Naren's first visit to Dakshineswar, he said: 'Naren entered the room by the western door, the one that faces the Ganga. I noticed that he had no concern about his bodily appearance; his hair and his clothes weren't tidy at all. He seemed altogether unattached, as if nothing external appealed to him. His eyes showed that the greater part of his mind was turned inward, all of the time. When I saw this, I marvelled to myself, "How is it possible that such a great spiritual aspirant can live in Calcutta, the home of the worldly-minded?"

'There was a mat spread out on the floor. I asked him to sit, and he sat down near the jar of Ganga water. A few of his friends were also with him that day. I saw that their nature was that of ordinary worldly people, just the opposite of his. They were thinking only of their pleasure.

'I asked him about his singing, and I found that he knew only two or three songs in Bengali. I asked him to sing them. He began singing the Brahmo song:

O mind, let us go home—
Why do you roam the world, that foreign land,
And wear its alien garb?

'He sang that song with his whole soul, as though he were deep in meditation. When I heard it, I couldn't control myself. I went into ecstasy.'

Naren has described the amazing scene which immediately followed:]

As soon as I had finished that song, the Master stood up, took me by the hand and led me on to the northern veranda. It was winter, so the open spaces between the pillars were covered with screens of matting to keep out the north wind; and this meant that, when the door of the room was closed, anyone standing on the veranda was hidden from both inside and outside. As soon as we were on the veranda, the Master closed the door. I thought he must be going to give me some instruction in private. But what he said and did next was something I could never have believed possible. He suddenly caught hold of my hand and began shedding tears of joy. He said to me affectionately as if to a familiar friend: 'You've come so late! Was that right? Couldn't you have guessed how I've been waiting for you? My ears are nearly burned off, listening to the talk of these worldly people. I thought I should burst, not having anyone to tell how I really felt!' He went on like that—raving and weeping. And then suddenly he folded his palms together and began addressing me as if I was some divine being, 'I know who you are, My Lord. You are Nara, the ancient sage, the incarnation of

Narayana. You have come back to earth to take away the sufferings and sorrows of mankind.' I was absolutely dumbfounded. I said to myself: 'What kind of a man is this? He must be raving mad! How can he talk like this to me, who am nobody— the son of Vishwanath Datta?' But I didn't answer him, and I let this wonderful madman go on talking as he chose. Presently he asked me to stay there on the veranda, and he went back into the room and came out again bringing butter, rock candy and a few pieces of sandesh; and then he began feeding me with his own hands. I kept asking him to give me the sweetmeats, so I could share them with my friends, but he wouldn't. 'They'll get some later,' he said, 'you take these for yourself.' And he wouldn't be satisfied until I'd eaten all of them. Then he took my hand and said, 'Promise me— you'll come back here soon, alone.' I couldn't refuse his request; it was made so earnestly. So I had to say, 'I will.' Then I went back into the room with him and sat down beside my friends.

'Here is a true man of renunciation,' I said to myself; 'he practises what he preaches; he has given up everything for God.' 'God can be seen and spoken to,' he told us, 'just as I'm seeing you and speaking to you. But who wants to see and speak to God? People grieve and shed enough tears to fill many pots, because their wives or their sons are dead, or because they've lost their money and their estates. But who weeps because he can't see God? And yet— if anyone really wants to see God, and if he calls upon him—God will reveal himself, that's certain.'

When I heard these words, I became more and more convinced that he wasn't like any of the other teachers of religion I had met—full of poetic talk and fine figures of speech—but that he was talking of what he directly knew, of what he himself had actually obtained, by giving up everything and by calling on God with his whole heart and strength. I thought, 'Well, he may be mad—but this is indeed a rare soul who can undertake such renunciation. Yes, he *is* mad—but how pure! And what renunciation! He is truly worthy of reverence.' Thinking this, I bowed down before his feet, took my leave of him and returned to Calcutta that day.

*   *   *

[Naren's description of his second visit to Dakshineswar. This time, he had to go the whole way there on foot.]

I had no idea that the Dakshineswar Temple was so far from Calcutta, because I had been there only once before and that was in a carriage. This time, it seemed as if the journey would never end, however far I walked. But, after asking many people the way, I arrived at Dakshineswar at last and went straight to the Master's room. I found him sitting, deep in his own meditations, on the smaller bed which stands beside the bigger one. There was no one with him. As soon as he saw me, he called me joyfully to him and made me sit down on one end of the bed. He was in a strange mood. He muttered something to himself which I couldn't understand, looked hard at me, then rose and approached me. I thought we were about to have another crazy scene. Scarcely had that thought passed through my mind before he placed his right foot on my body. Immediately, I had a wonderful experience. My eyes were wide open, and I saw that everything in the room, including the walls themselves, was whirling rapidly around and receding, and at the same time, it seemed to me that my consciousness of self, together with the entire universe, was about to vanish into a vast, all-devouring void. This destruction of my consciousness of self seemed to me to be the same thing as death. I felt that death was right before me, very close. Unable to control myself, I cried out loudly, 'Ah, what are you doing to me? Don't you know I have my parents at home?' When the Master heard this, he gave a loud laugh. Then, touching my chest with his hand, he said, 'All right—let it stop now. It needn't be done all at once. It will happen in its own good time.' To my amazement, this extraordinary vision of mine vanished as suddenly as it had come. I returned to my normal state and saw things inside and outside the room standing stationary, as before.

Although it has taken so much time to describe all this, it actually happened in only a few moments.

And yet it changed my whole way of thinking. I was bewildered and kept trying to analyse what had happened. I had seen how this experience had begun and ended in obedience to the will of this extraordinary man. I had read about hypnotism in books and I wondered if this was something of the same kind. But my heart refused to believe that it was. For even people of great will-power can only create such conditions when they are working on weak minds. And my mind was by no means weak. Up to then, in fact, I had been proud of my intelligence and will-power. This man did not bewitch me or reduce me to his puppet. On the contrary, when I first met him, I had decided that he was mad. Why then should I have suddenly found myself in this state? It seemed an utter mystery to me. But I determined to be on my guard, lest he should get further influence over me in the future.

(From *Ramakrishna and His Disciples*, pp. 192-98)

And yet it changed my whole way of thinking. I was
bewildered. I had seen how this experience had
happened. I had seen how this experience had

'RAMAKRISHNA DEDICATED ME'

I went about hither and thither in search of a
job even before the period of mourning [due to the
passing away of his father] was over. Suffering from
lack of food, I was going barefooted from office to
office with an application for a job in my hand in
the blazing midday sun. Sympathising with me in
my sorrow, some of my very intimate friends would
be with me some days, but on other days they
could not be. But I had to be disappointed everywhere. From that very first worldly experience of
mine I felt keenly that selfless sympathy was very
rare in this world—there was no place here for the
weak and the poor. Those who deemed it, only a
day or two previously, a piece of good fortune to be
able to help me now found an opportunity to do
the contrary and made a wry face at me and,
although able, were reluctant to help me. When I
had such experiences, the world seemed to me, very
often, to have been created by a demon. One day,
at that time, when I was going from place to place
in the sun, my sole, I remember, was blistered. Extremely fatigued, I had to sit down in the shade of
the Ochterloney monument in the Maidan. A
friend or two were with me that day or met me
there by chance. One of them, I remember distinctly, sang by way of consoling me—

'Here blows the wind, the breath of Brahman,
His grace palpable....'

When I heard the song I felt as if he was inflicting severe blows on my head. Remembering the sheer helpless condition of my mother and brothers, I blurted out in resentment, despair and disappointment, 'Shut up. Those who are in the lap of luxury or do not know what the pinch of hunger means, and whose nearest and dearest ones are not starving and going naked—to such people, in the midst of the fullest enjoyment of life, such flights of imagination appear sweet and pleasing. I also had such days and felt similarly, but now, confronted with stern reality, all these sentiments seem to be a terrible mockery.'

In spite of all my trials, my faith in the existence of God did not vanish so long, for all that pain and misery, nor did I doubt that 'God is good.' I used to wake up from sleep in the morning, remembered the Lord and left my bed taking His name. Then with firm determination and hope I went from place to place in search of some means of earning money. I was leaving my bed as usual, calling on the Lord, when one day, my mother heard my words from the adjacent room and suddenly said, 'Stop, lad; you have been constantly repeating the name of the divine Lord ever since your childhood—and your divine Lord has left nothing undone!' The words hurt me terribly. Cut to the quick, I pondered, 'Does God actually exist? If so, does He hear the plaintive prayer of man? Why is there then no response to so much of prayer which I proffer to Him? Whence is so much of evil in the creation of a

6

benign Creator? Why is there so much of calamity in the kingdom of one who is all Bliss?'...My heart was pierced through by a feeling of wounded love; and doubt in the existence of God assailed me.

It was against my nature to do anything and conceal it from others. Never from my childhood could I conceal, out of fear or from any other motive, even the least shade of thought, let alone my actions. Was it, therefore, surprising that I should now go aggressively forward to prove to the people that God did not exist and, even if he did, there was no need to call on Him, for it produced no result to do so. Consequently, a rumour soon spread that I had become an atheist and was mixing with people of bad character, did not shrink from drinking and even from frequenting the houses of ill-fame.

News travels from ear to ear. It did not take long for those words of mine to get variously distorted and reach the Master's ears at Dakshineswar and those of his devotees in Calcutta. Some came to see me with a view to ascertaining the real state I was in, and let me know by signs and gestures that they were ready to believe something at least, if not all, of what they had heard. Knowing that they could regard me so low, I became terribly wounded at heart and proved that it was a great weakness to believe in God for fear of being punished. And quoting Hume, Mill, Bain, Comte and other western philosophers, I started a fierce argumentation with them to prove that there was no evidence of the existence of God. Consequently, they went away, as I came to know afterwards, far more convinced of my fall than ever before. I was happy to know that and I thought that the Master would hear of it from them and would perhaps believe it too. The moment this thought crossed my mind, my heart was filled with a tragic wounded feeling. I came to the conclusion that there was no harm if he did so, inasmuch as people's opinions, good and bad, were worth so little. Later, however, I was surprised to hear that the Master had heard of it all from them but had not expressed himself either way at first; but when afterwards Bhavanath wept and said to him, 'Sir, it was beyond even our dream that such would be Narendranath's lot', he excitedly said, 'Silence! you rascals! He, Mother has told me, can never be such; if you mention it again to me I'll not be able to put up with your presence.'

I became absolutely indifferent to the praise or blame of the world. And, firmly convinced that I was not born to earn money, serve the family and spend time in worldly enjoyment like the people in general, I was secretly getting ready to renounce the world like my grandfather. When the day for starting on my itineracy was fixed, I heard the news that the Master would come to a devotee's house at Calcutta that day. I thought it was very good; I would see the Guru before I renounced home for ever. As soon as I met the Master, he importunately said to me, 'You must come to Dakshineswar with me today.' I offered various excuses, but he was inexorable. I had to drive with him. There was not

much talk in the carriage. After reaching Dakshineswar I sat with others in his room for some time,
when the Master entered into Bhavasamadhi. In a
moment he came suddenly to me and, taking my
hand in his, began singing as tears flowed:

> I am afraid to speak
> And am equally afraid not to speak.
> The doubt rises in my mind
> Lest I should lose you.
> (Ah my Rai![1] lest I lose you.)

I long kept back the surge of the strong emotions
of my mind but could no more check their force.
My breast too was flooded with tears like that of the
Master. I was quite sure that the Master knew
everything. All the others were astonished to see
that behaviour of ours. Some asked the Master the
reason for this after he came back to the normal
state, when he smiled and answered, 'It is something
between ourselves'. Afterwards, sending away all
others, he called me to him at night and said, 'I
know, you have come to the world for Mother's
work, you can never live a worldly life. But remain
in your family for my sake as long as I live.' Saying
so, the Master immediately began shedding tears
again with his voice choked with emotion!

I bade good-bye to the Master and returned

---

[1] There is a pun on the two words 'ha rai'; when separate
they mean Ah! Rai (Radha); and when not, they mean,
'lest I should lose'.

home the next day. And immediately, a hundred
thoughts about the family occupied my mind. I
began going from place to place now as before and
made various kinds of efforts. I worked in the office
of the attorney and translated a few books, as a
result of which I earned a little money and the
household was being managed somehow. But these
were all temporary jobs; and in the absence of any
permanent work no smooth arrangement for the
maintenance of mother and brothers could be
made. I remembered a little later: 'God grants the
Master's prayers. I shall make him pray for me so
that the suffering of my mother and brothers for
want of food and clothing might be removed; he
will never refuse to do so for my sake.' I hurried to
Dakshineswar and asked persistently that he must
pray to the Mother that the pecuniary difficulty of
my mother and brothers might be removed. The
Master said to me affectionately, 'My child, I
cannot say such words, you know. Why don't you
yourself pray? You don't accept the Mother; that
is why you suffer so much.' I replied, 'I have no
knowledge of the Mother; please pray to Mother
yourself for my sake. Pray you must; I will not leave
you unless you do so.' The Master said with affec-
tion, 'I prayed to Mother many times indeed to
remove your sufferings. But as you do not accept
Mother, She does not grant the prayer. Well, today
is Tuesday, a day especially sacred to Mother.
Mother will, I say, grant you whatever you would
ask for. Go to the temple tonight and, bowing down

to Her, pray for a boon. My affectionate Mother is the Power of Brahman; She is pure Consciousness embodied. She has given birth to the universe according to Her will; what can She not do, if She wills?'

A firm faith arose in my mind that all the sufferings would certainly come to an end as soon as I prayed to the Mother, inasmuch as the Master had said so. I waited for the night in great expectancy. The night arrived at last. Three hours of the night had elapsed when the Master asked me to go to the holy temple. As I was going, a sort of profound inebriation possessed me; I was reeling. A firm conviction gripped me that I should actually see Mother and hear Her words. I forgot all other things, and became completely merged in that thought alone. Coming in the temple, I saw that Mother was actually pure Consciousness, was actually living and was really the fountain-head of infinite love and beauty. My heart swelled with loving devotion; and, beside myself with bliss, I made repeated salutations to Her, praying, 'Mother, grant me discrimination, grant me detachment, grant me divine knowledge and devotion; ordain that I may always have unobstructed vision of you.' My heart was flooded with peace. The whole universe completely disappeared and Mother alone remained filling my heart.

No sooner had I returned to the Master than he asked, 'Did you pray to Mother for the removal of your worldly wants?' Startled at his question, I said, 'No, sir; I forgot to do so. So, what should I do now?' He said, 'Go quickly again and pray to Her.' I started for the temple once more, and, coming to Mother's presence, became inebriated again. I forgot everything, bowed down to Her repeatedly and prayed for the realization of divine knowledge and devotion, before I came back. The Master smiled and said, 'Well, did you tell Her this time?' I was startled again and said, 'No, sir; hardly had I seen Mother when I forgot everything on account of the influence of an indescribable divine Power and prayed for knowledge and devotion only. What's to be done now?' The Master said, 'Silly boy, could you not control yourself a little and make that prayer? Go once more, if you can and tell Her those words. Quick!' I started a third time; but as soon as I entered the temple a formidable sense of shame occupied my heart. I thought what a trifling thing have I come to ask of Mother? It is, as the Master says, just like the folly of asking a king, having received his grace, for gourds and pumpkins. Ah! how low is my intellect! Overpowered with shame and aversion I bowed down to Her over and over again saying, 'I don't want anything else, Mother; do grant me divine knowledge and devotion only.' When I came out from the temple, it occurred to me that it was certainly the play of the Master, otherwise how was it that I could not speak the words though I came to pray to Her as many as three times? Afterwards I insisted that he must ensure my mother's and brothers' freedom from lack of food and clothing, saying, 'It is certainly you who made me intoxicated that way.' He said affectionately to me, 'My child, I can never offer such a prayer for anyone; it does not indeed come out of my mouth. You would, I told you, get from Mother whatever you wanted. But you could not ask Her for it; you are not meant for worldly happiness. What am I to do?' I said, 'That won't do, sir. You must utter the prayer for my sake; it is my firm conviction that they will be free from all sufferings if you only say so.' As I kept on persisting, he said, 'Well, they will never be in want of plain food and clothing.'

(From *Sri Ramakrishna The Great Master*, pp. 806-12)

*   *   *

Swamiji: I used to hate Kali and all Her ways. *That* was my six years' fight, because I would not accept Kali.

Nivedita: But now you have accepted Her specially, have you not, Swami?

Swamiji: I had to. Ramakrishna Paramahamsa dedicated me to Her. And you know I believe that she guides me in every little thing I do, and just does what She likes with me. Yet I fought so long. I loved the man, you see, and that held me. I thought him the purest man I had ever seen, and I know that he loved me as my own father and mother had not the power to do.

Nivedita: But when you doubted so long, with all your chances, what wonder if Brahmos still doubt?

Swamiji: Yes, but they never saw that immense purity in Him that I saw!...nor got the love.

Nivedita: But I fancy it was His greatness that made the love hold you without palling—wasn't it?

Swamiji: His greatness had not dawned on me then. That was afterwards, when I had given in. At that time I thought Him simply a brain-sick baby, always seeing visions and things. I hated it. And then *I* had to accept Her too!

Nivedita: Won't you tell me what made you do that, Swami? What broke all your opposition down?

Swamiji: No, that will die with me. I had great misfortunes at that time, you know. My father died, and so on. And She saw Her opportunity to make a slave of me. They were His very words: 'To make a slave of you.' And Ramakrishna Paramahamsa made me over to Her.... Curious, He only lived two years after doing that, and most of that time He was suffering. He was only six months in His own health and brightness.

Nivedita: I always look upon Sri Ramakrishna as an Incarnation of Kali. Isn't that what the future will call Him?

Swamiji: Yes, I think there's no doubt that Kali worked up the body of Ramakrishna for Her own ends.

(Excerpt from Sister Nivedita's diary, reproduced in *Nivedita Lokamata*, pp. 320-21)

AT THE FEET OF MY MASTER

When I was a boy here, in this city of Calcutta, I used to go from place to place in search of religion, and everywhere I asked the lecturer after hearing very big lectures, 'Have you seen God?' The man was taken aback at the idea of seeing God; and the only man who told me, 'I have', was Ramakrishna Paramahamsa, and not only so, but he said, 'I will put you in the way of seeing Him too.' (III. 345-46)

Ay, where would I have been, if I had not been blessed with the dust of the holy feet of that orthodox, image-worshipping Brahmin! (III. 460)

Sir, granted that Ramakrishna Paramahamsa was a sham, granted that it has been a very serious mistake, indeed, to take refuge in him, but what is the way out now? What if one life is spent in vain, but shall a *man* eat his own words? Can there be such a thing as having a dozen husbands? Any of you may join any party you like, I have no objection, no, not in the least, but travelling this world over I find that save and except his circle alone, everywhere else thought and act are at variance. For those that belong to him, I have the utmost love, the utmost confidence. I have no alternative in the matter. Call me one-sided if you will, but there you have my *bona fide* avowal. If but a thorn pricks the foot of one who has surrendered himself to Sri Ramakrishna, it makes my bones ache. All others I love; you will find very few men so unsectarian as I am; but you must excuse me, I have that bit of bigotry. If I do not appeal to his name, whose else shall I? It will be time enough to seek for a big Guru in our next birth; but in this, it is that unlearned Brahmin who has bought this body of mine for ever. (VI. 345-46)

Never during his life did he refuse a single prayer of mine: millions of offences has he forgiven me; such great love even my parents never had for me. (VI. 232)

The man at whose feet I sat all my life—and it is only a few ideas of his that I try to teach—could [hardly] write his name at all. All my life I have not seen another man like that, and I have travelled all over the world. When I think of that man, I feel like a fool, because I want to read books and he never did. He never wanted to lick the plates after other people had eaten. That is why he was his own book. (VI. 64)

One time Swamiji said, 'I am the disciple of a man who could not write his own name, but I am not worthy to unloose his shoes. How often I have wished that I could take this intellect and throw it in the Ganga.'

'But Swami,' protested one woman, 'your intellect is what we like about you.' 'That is because you are a fool, Madame, as I am,' was Swamiji's answer. (*Reminiscences of Swami Vivekananda*, p. 388)

You see, the fact is that Sri Ramakrishna is not exactly what the ordinary followers have comprehended him to be. He had infinite moods and phases. Even if you might form an idea of the limits of Brahmajnana, the knowledge of the Absolute, you could not have any idea of the unfathomable depths of his mind! Thousands of Vivekanandas may spring forth through one gracious glance of his eyes!...Time and again have I received in this life marks of his grace. He stands behind and gets all this work done by me. When lying helpless under a tree in an agony of hunger, when I had not even a scrap of cloth for Kaupina, when I was resolved on travelling penniless round the world, even then help came in all ways by the grace of Sri Ramakrishna. And again when crowds jostled with one another in the streets of Chicago to have a sight of this Vivekananda, then also, just because I had his grace, I could digest without difficulty all that honour—a hundredth part of which would have been enough to turn mad any ordinary man—because I had his grace; and by his will, victory followed everywhere. (VI. 479, 478)

I went to Sri Ramakrishna and I loved the man, but I hated all his ideas. And so for six years it was hard fighting all the time. I would say, 'I don't care in the least for this thing you want me to do',

and he would say, 'Never mind, just do it, and you
will see that certain results follow.' And all that
time he gave me such love; no one has ever given
me such love, and there was so much reverence
with it. He used to think, 'This boy will be So-and-
so', I suppose, and he would never let me do any
menial service for him. He kept that up to the very
moment of his death too. He wouldn't let me fan
him, and many other things he would not let me
do. (*Reminiscences of Swami Vivekananda*, p. 277)

Two or three days before Sri Ramakrishna's
passing away, he called me to his side one day, and
asking me to sit before him, looked steadfastly at
me and fell into Samadhi. Then I really felt that
a subtle force like an electric shock was entering
my body! In a little while, I also lost outward
consciousness and sat motionless. How long I stayed
in that condition I do not remember; when consciousness returned I found Sri Ramakrishna
shedding tears. On questioning him, he answered
me affectionately, 'Today, giving you my all, I
have become a beggar. With this power you are
to do many works for the world's good before you
will return.' I feel that that power is constantly
directing me to this or that work. This body has
not been made for remaining idle. (VII. 206-07)

Sri Ramakrishna said to me: 'Wherever you will
take me on your shoulders, there I will go and stay,
be it under a tree or in a hut.' It is therefore that I

am myself carrying him on my shoulders to the new Math grounds (Belur Math). Know it for certain that Sri Ramakrishna will keep his seat fixed there, for the welfare of the many, for a long time to come. (VII. 114)

I am a disciple of Ramakrishna Paramahamsa, a perfect Sannyasin whose influence and ideas I fell under. This great Sannyasin never assumed the negative or critical attitude towards other religions, but showed their positive side—how they could be carried into life and practised. To fight, to assume the antagonistic attitude, is the exact contrary of his teaching, which dwells on the truth that the world is moved by love. (V. 190)

I have already told you at the outset that I am Ramakrishna's slave, having laid my body at his feet 'with Til and Tulasi leaves', I cannot disregard his behest. If it is in failure that that great sage laid down his life after having attained to super-human heights of Jnana, Bhakti, Love, and powers, and after having practised for forty years stern renunciation, non-attachment, holiness, and great austerities, then where is there anything for us to count on? So I am obliged to trust his words as the words of one identified with truth.

Now his behest to me was that I should devote myself to the service of the order of all-renouncing devotees founded by him, and in this I have to persevere, come what may, being ready to take heaven, hell, salvation, or anything that may happen to me.....If you ask, 'You are a Sannyasin, so why do you trouble over these desires?'—I would then reply, I am Ramakrishna's servant, and I am willing even to steal and rob, if by doing so I can perpetuate his name in the land of his birth and Sadhana (spiritual struggle) and help even a little his disciples to practise his great ideals. (VI. 239-41)

Question: What induced you to forsake the ordinary course of the world, Swami?

Swamiji: I had a deep interest in religion and philosophy from my childhood, and our books teach renunciation as the highest ideal to which man can aspire. It only needed the meeting with a great Teacher—Ramakrishna Paramahamsa—to kindle in me the final determination to follow the path he himself had trod, as in him I found my highest ideal realized.

Question: Then did he found a sect, which you now represent?

Swamiji: No, his whole life was spent in breaking down the barriers of sectarianism and dogma. He formed no sect. Quite the reverse. He advocated and strove to establish absolute freedom of thought. He was a great Yogi. (V. 186)

*   *   *

After all, I am only the boy who used to listen

with rapt wonderment to the wonderful words of
Ramakrishna under the Banyan at Dakshineswar.
That is my true nature; works and activities, doing
good and so forth are all superimpositions. Now I
again hear his voice; the same old voice thrilling
my soul. Bonds are breaking—love dying, work
becoming tasteless—the glamour is off life. Only
the voice of the Master calling.—'I come Lord, I
come.' 'Let the dead bury the dead, follow thou
Me.'—'I come, my beloved Lord, I come.' Nirvana
is before me. I feel it at times—the same infinite
ocean of peace, without a ripple, a breath.

(VI. 431-32)

APPENDIX

7

Thy servant am I through birth after birth,
Sea of mercy, inscrutable Thy ways;
So is my destiny inscrutable;
It is unknown; nor would I wish to know.
Bhakti, Mukti, Japa, Tapas, all these,
Enjoyment, worship, and devotion too—
These things and all things similar to these,
I have expelled at Thy supreme command.
But only one desire is left in me—
An intimacy with Thee, mutual!
    Take me, O Lord, across to Thee;
    Let no desire's dividing line prevent.

Thou art my Master! Thou my soul's real mate.
Many a time I see Thee—I am Thee!
Ay! I am Thee, and Thou, my Lord, art me!
Thou art my voice. Within my throat,
As Vinapani,[1] art Thou.

(IV. 511-12)

[1] Goddess of Learning

CONVERSATIONS WITH RAMAKRISHNA
(*Extracts*)

5 *March* 1882

Sri Ramakrishna was sitting on the small couch. The room was filled with devotees, who had taken advantage of the holiday to come to see the Master. M. (Mahendra Nath Gupta: the author of *The Gospel of Sri Ramakrishna*) had not yet become acquainted with any of them; so he took his seat in a corner.

He (Ramakrishna) addressed his words particularly to a young man of nineteen, named Narendranath, who was a college student and frequented the Sadharan Brahmo Samaj. His eyes were bright, his words were full of spirit, and he had the look of a lover of God.

M. guessed that the conversation was about worldly men, who look down on those who aspire to spiritual things. The Master was talking about the great number of such people in the world, and about how to deal with them.

Master (*to Narendra*): How do you feel about it? Worldly people say all kinds of things about the spiritually minded. But look here! When an elephant moves along the street, any number of curs and other small animals may bark and cry after it; but the elephant doesn't even look back at them. If people speak ill of you, what will you think of them?

Narendra: I shall think that dogs are barking at me.

Master (smiling): Oh, no! You mustn't go that far, my child! *(Laughter)*. God dwells in all beings. But you may be intimate only with good people; you must keep away from the evil-minded. God is even in the tiger; but you cannot embrace the tiger on that account. You may say, 'Why run away from a tiger, which is also a manifestation of God?' The answer to that is: Those who tell you to run away are also manifestations of God—and why shouldn't you listen to them?

Pointing to Narendra, the Master said: You all see this boy. He behaves that way here. A naughty boy seems very gentle when with his father. But he is quite another person when he plays in the Chandni. Narendra and people of his type belong to the class of the ever-free. They are never entangled in the world. When they grow a little older they feel the awakening of inner consciousness and go directly toward God. They come to the world only to teach others. They never care for anything of the world. They are never attached to 'woman and gold'.

At this point Narendra left the room.

Master: You see, Narendra excels in singing, playing on instruments, study and everything. The other day he had a discussion with Kedar and tore his arguments to shreds. *(All laugh.)*

19 *August* 1883

M. accompanied the Master to the veranda,

where Narendra was talking with Hazra. Sri
Ramakrishna knew that Hazra always indulged
in dry philosophical discussions. Hazra would say:
The world is unreal, like a dream. Worship, food
offerings to the Deity, and so forth, are only hallucinations of the mind. The aim of spiritual life
is to meditate on one's own real self. Then he
would repeat: 'I am He.' But with all that, he had
a soft corner in his heart for money, material things,
and people's attention.

Sri Ramakrishna smiled and said to Hazra and
Narendra: Hello! What are you talking about?

Narendra (smiling): Oh, we are discussing a great
many things. They are rather too deep for others.

Master (with a smile): But Pure Knowledge and
Pure Love are one and the same thing. Both lead
the aspirants to the same goal. The path of love is
much the easier.

Narendra quoted a song:

O Mother, make me mad with Thy love!
What need have I of knowledge or reason?

Narendra said to M. that he had been reading
a book by Hamilton, who wrote: 'A learned ignorance is the end of philosophy and the beginning
of religion.'

Master (to M.): What does that mean?

Narendra explained the sentence in Bengali.
The Master beamed with joy and said in English,
'Thank you! Thank you!' Everyone laughed at the
charming way he said these words. They knew

that his English vocabulary consisted of only half
a dozen words.

25 *June* 1884

Master: I say to you, dive deep in God-con-
sciousness.

Saying this, the Master began to sing in an
ecstasy of love for God:

> Dive deep, O mind, dive deep in the Ocean
>   of God's Beauty;
> If you descend to the uttermost depths,
> There you will find the gem of love....

The Master continued: One does not die if one
sinks in this Ocean. This is the Ocean of Immortal-
ity. Once I said to Narendra: 'God is the Ocean of
Bliss. Tell me if you want to plunge into It. Just
imagine there is some syrup in a cup and that you
have become a fly. Now tell me where you will sit
to sip the syrup.' Narendra answered: 'I will sit
on the edge of the cup and stretch out my neck to
drink, because I am sure to die if I go far into the
cup.' Then I said to him: 'But my child, this is the
Ocean of Satchidananda. There is no fear of death
in It. This is the Ocean of Immortality. Only
ignorant people say that one should not have an
excess of devotion and divine love. How foolish!
Can there be any excess of divine love?'

22 *February* 1885

Sri Ramakrishna was sitting on the north-east

veranda outside his room at Dakshineswar. It was about eight o'clock in the morning.

Narendra had been talking a long time with Hazra on the porch. Since his father's death Narendra had been having financial worries. He entered the room and took a seat.

Master (to Narendra): Were you with Hazra? Both of you are in the same boat. You know the saying about the two friends: You are away from your country and he is away from his beloved. Hazra, too, needs fifteen hundred rupees. (*Laughter.*) Hazra says: Narendra has acquired one hundred per cent Sattva, though still there is in him a pink glow of Rajas. But I have one hundred and twenty-five per cent pure Sattva. (*All laugh.*)

Narendra and many other devotees were seated on the floor. Girish entered the room and joined them.

Master (to Girish): I look on Narendra as Atman. I obey him.

Girish: Is there anyone you don't obey?

Master (smiling): He has a manly nature and I have the nature of a woman. He is a noble soul and belongs to the realm of the Indivisible Brahman.

Girish went out to have a smoke.

Narendra (to the Master): I had a talk with Girish Ghosh. He is indeed a great man. We talked about you.

Master: What did you say about me?

Narendra: That you are illiterate and we are scholars. Oh, we talked in that vein! (*Laughter.*)

Mani Mallick (to the Master): You have become a pandit without reading a book.

Master (to Narendra and the others): Let me tell you this: really and truly I don't feel sorry in the least that I haven't read the Vedanta or the other scriptures. I know that the essence of the Vedanta is that Brahman alone is real and the world illusory. And what is the essence of the *Gita*? It is what you get by repeating the word ten times. Then it is reversed into 'tagi', which refers to renunciation.

25 *February* 1885

Sri Ramakrishna arrived at the Star Theatre, on Beadon Street, to see a performance of Vrishaketu.* He sat in a box, facing the south. M. and other devotees were near him.

Master (to M.): Has Narendra come?

M.: Yes, sir.

After the play Sri Ramakrishna went to the recreation room of the theatre. Girish and Narendra were already there. The Master stood near Narendra and said: I have come.

Master (to Girish): Does this theatre belong to you?

Girish: It is *ours*, sir.

Master: 'Ours' is good; it is not good to say 'mine'. People say 'I' and 'mine'; they are egotistic, small-minded people.

Narendra: The whole world is a theatre.

---

* Vrishaketu was the son of Karna, a hero of the *Mahabharata*, who was celebrated alike for charity and heroism. Karna sacrificed his son to fulfil a promise.

Master: Yes, yes, that's right. In some places you see the play of Vidya and in some, the play of Avidya.

Narendra: Everything is the play of Vidya.

Master: True, true. But a man realizes that when he has the Knowledge of Brahman. But for a Bhakta who follows the path of divine love, both exist —Vidyamaya and Avidyamaya. Please sing a little.

Narendra sang:

Upon the Sea of Blissful Awareness waves of
    ecstatic love arise:
Rapture divine! Play of God's Bliss!
Oh, how enthralling!

11 *March* 1885

Many of his devotees were in the room. Narendra did not believe that God could incarnate Himself in a human body. But Girish differed with him; he had the burning faith that from time to time the Almighty Lord, through His inscrutable Power, assumes a human body and descends to earth to serve a divine purpose.

The Master said to Girish: I should like to hear you and Narendra argue in English.

The discussion began; but they talked in Bengali.

Narendra: God is Infinity. How is it possible for us to comprehend Him? He dwells in every human being. It is not the case that he manifests Himself through one person only.

Sri Ramakrishna (*tenderly*): I quite agree with

Narendra. God is everywhere. But then you must
remember that there are different manifestations
of His Power in different beings. At some places
there is a manifestation of His Avidyashakti, at
others a manifestation of His Vidyashakti. Through
different instruments God's Power is manifest in
different degrees, greater and smaller. Therefore
all men are not equal.

Ram: What is the use of these futile arguments?

Master (sharply): No! No! There is a meaning in
all this.

Girish (to Narendra): How do you know that God
does not assume a human body?

Narendra: God is 'beyond words or thought'.

Master: No, that is not true. He can be known by
the pure Buddhi, which is the same as the Pure
Self. The seers of old directly perceived the Pure
Self through their pure Buddhi.

Girish (to Narendra): Unless God Himself teaches
men through His human Incarnation, who else
will teach them spiritual mysteries? God takes a
human body to teach men divine knowledge and
divine love. Otherwise, who will teach?

Narendra: Why, God dwells in our own heart; He
will certainly teach us from within the heart.

Master (tenderly): Yes, yes. He will teach us as our
Inner Guide....I clearly see that God is every-
thing; He Himself has become all....Shankara's
Non-dualistic explanation of Vedanta is true, and
so is the Qualified Non-dualistic interpretation of
Ramanuja.

Narendra: What is Qualified Non-dualism?

Master: It is the theory of Ramanuja. According to this theory, Brahman, or the Absolute, is qualified by the universe and its living beings. These three—Brahman, the world, and living beings—together constitute One.

Narendra was sitting beside the Master. He touched Narendra's body and said: As long as a man argues about God, he has not realized Him. The nearer you approach to God, the less you reason and argue. When you attain Him, then all sounds—all reasoning and disputing—come to an end. Then you go into Samadhi—sleep—into communion with God in silence.

4 January 1886

[Sri Ramakrishna had been moved to a beautiful house at Cossipore.] Narendra arrived. Now and then the Master looked at him and smiled.

Narendra: I have been thinking of going there today.

Master: Where?

Narendra: To Dakshineswar. I intend to light a fire under the bel-tree and meditate.

Master: No, the authorities of the powder-magazine will not allow it. The Panchavati is a nice place. Many sadhus have practised Japa and meditation there. But it is very cold there. The place is dark, too.

Again for a few moments all sat in silence.

Master (to Narendra, smiling): Won't you continue your studies?

Narendra (*looking at the Master and M.*): I shall feel greatly relieved if I find a medicine that will make me forget all I have studied.

It was evening. Narendra was sitting in a room downstairs. He was smoking and describing to M. the yearning of his soul. No one else was with them.

Narendra: I was meditating here last Saturday when suddenly I felt a peculiar sensation in my heart.

M.: It was the awakening of the Kundalini.

Narendra: Probably it was. I clearly perceived the Ida and the Pingala nerves. I asked Hazra to feel my chest. Yesterday I saw him (meaning the Master) upstairs and told him about it. I said to him: 'All the others have had their realization; please give me some. All have succeeded; shall I alone remain unsatisfied?'

M.: What did he say to you?

Narendra: He said, 'Why don't you settle your family affairs first and then come to me? You will get everything. What do you want?' I replied, 'It is my desire to remain absorbed in Samadhi continually for three or four days, only once in a while coming down to the sense plane to eat a little food.' Thereupon he said to me: 'You are a very small-minded person. There is a state higher even than that. "All that exists art Thou"—it is you who sing that song.'

M.: Yes, he always says that after coming down from Samadhi one sees that it is God Himself who has become the universe, the living beings, and all that exists. The Ishvarakotis alone can attain that state.

Narendra: I have no more taste for the world. I do not relish the company of those who live in the world—of course, with the exception of one or two devotees.

Narendra became silent again. A fire of intense renunciation was burning within him. His soul was restless for the vision of God. He resumed the conversation.

Narendra (*to M.*): You have found peace, but my soul is restless. You are blessed indeed.

M. did not reply, but sat in silence. Immediately after dusk M. went upstairs. Niranjan and Shashi were sitting near the Master. Every now and then he talked of Narendra.

Master: How wonderful Narendra's state of mind is! You see, this very Narendra did not believe in the forms of God. And now you see how his soul is panting for God! When the soul longs and yearns for God, then you will know that you do not have long to wait for His vision. The rosy colour on the eastern horizon shows that the sun will soon rise.

At night Narendra left for Dakshineswar.

15 *March* 1886

About seven o'clock in the morning Sri Ramakrishna felt a little better. He talked to the devotees, sometimes in a whisper, sometimes by signs.... The Master looks at the devotees and his love for them wells up in a thousand streams. Like a mother showing her tenderness to her children he touches the faces and chins of Rakhal and Narendra.

He says to M.: If the body were to be preserved a few days more, many people would have their spirituality awakened....

But this is not to be. This time the body will not be preserved.

Rakhal (*tenderly*): Please speak to God that He may preserve your body some time more.

Master: That depends on God's will.

Narendra: Your will and God's will have become one.

Sri Ramakrishna remains silent. Pausing a few moments he says: A band of minstrels suddenly appears, dances, and sings, and it departs in the same sudden manner. They come and they return, but none recognizes them.

Sri Ramakrishna looks at Narendra very tenderly.

Master (*to Narendra*): An outcaste was carrying a load of meat. Shankaracharya, after bathing in the Ganga, was passing by. Suddenly the outcaste touched him. Shankara said sharply: 'What! You touched me!' 'Revered sir,' he replied: 'I have not touched you nor have you touched me. Reason with me: Are you the body, the mind, or the Buddhi? Analyse what you are. You are the Pure Atman, unattached and free, unaffected by the three Gunas—Sattva, Rajas, and Tamas.'

Do you know what Brahman is like? It is like

air. Good and bad smells are carried by the air, but the air itself is unaffected.

Narendra: Yes, sir.

Master: He is beyond both the Maya of knowledge and the Maya of ignorance. 'Woman and gold' is the Maya of ignorance. Knowledge, renunciation, devotion, and other spiritual qualities are the splendours of the Maya of knowledge.

Narendra: Some people get angry with me when I speak of renunciation.

Master (in a whisper): Renunciation is necessary. If one thing is placed upon another, you must remove the one to get the other. Can you get the second thing without removing the first?

Narendra: True, sir.

The Master looks at Narendra tenderly and becomes filled with love. Looking at the devotees, he says: Grand!

Narendra asks the Master: What is grand?

Master (smiling): I see that preparations are going on for a grand renunciation.

Rakhal: Narendra is now beginning to understand you rather well.

Master (smiling to Narendra): Well, what do you think of me?

Narendra: You are a hero, a handmaid of God and everything else.

These words fill Sri Ramakrishna with divine emotion. He places his hand on his heart and says: I see that all things—everything that exists—have come from this.

He asks Narendra by a sign: What did you understand?

Narendra:. All created objects have come from you.

9 *April* 1886

Master (*to Narendra*): Well, here you find every-thing—even ordinary red lentils and tamarind. Isn't that so?

Narendra: After experiencing all those states, you are now dwelling on a lower plane.

Master: Someone seems to be holding me to a lower plane.

Saying this, Sri Ramakrishna took the fan from M.'s hand and said: As I see this fan, *directly* before me, in exactly the same manner have I seen God. And I have seen that He and the one who dwells in my heart are one and the same Person.

Narendra: Yes, yes! 'Soham'—I am He.

Master: But only a line divides the two—that I may enjoy divine bliss.

Narendra (*to M.*): Great souls, even after their own liberation, retain the ego and experience the pleasure and pain of the body that they may help others to attain liberation.

Master: The roof is clearly visible; but it is extremely hard to reach it.

Narendra: Yes, sir.

Master: But if someone who has already reached it drops down a rope, he can pull another person up.

Rakhal: Let us stop here. He has already talked a great deal. It will aggravate his illness.

(From *The Gospel of Sri Ramakrishna*)

CONVERSATIONS WITH RAMAKRISHNA 187

Rakhal: Let us stop here. He has already talked

FURTHER GLIMPSES OF RAMAKRISHNA

[Sri Ramakrishna passed away on 16 August 1886, plung-
ing his devotees and disciples into a sea of grief. After a short
time Narendra, Rakhal, Niranjan, Sharat, Shashi, Baburam,
Jogin, Tarak, Kali, and Latu renounced the world for good.
Surendra, a householder disciple of Sri Ramakrishna, said
to the young disciples of the Master: 'Brothers, where will
you go? Let us rent a house. You will live there and make
it our Master's shrine; and we householders shall come there
for consolation. How can we pass all our days and nights with
our wives and children in the world? I used to spend a sum
of money for the Master at Cossipore. I shall gladly give it
now for your expenses.' Accordingly he rented a house for
them at Baranagore, and this place became gradually trans-
formed into a math or monastery.]

25 March 1887

M. arrived at the Baranagore Math to visit his
brother-disciples. He was very eager to observe
the spirit of intense renunciation of these young
men. It was evening. M. intended to spend the
night in the monastery.

When the worship was over, Narendra and M.
became engaged in conversation. Narendra was
recalling his various meetings with Sri Ramakrishna.

Narendra: One day, during one of my early
visits, the Master in an ecstatic mood said to me,
'You have come!' 'How amazing!' I said to myself.
'It is as if he had known me a long time.' Then
he said to me, 'Do you ever see light?' I replied:

Yes, sir. Before I fall asleep I feel something like a light revolving near my forehead.

M.: Do you see it even now?

Narendra: I used to see it frequently. In Jadu Mallick's garden house the Master one day touched me and muttered something to himself. I became unconscious. The effect of the touch lingered with me a month, like an intoxication.

When he heard that a proposal had been made about my marriage, he wept, holding the feet of the image of Kali. With tears in his eyes he prayed to the Divine Mother: O Mother, please upset the whole thing! Don't let Narendra be drowned.

After my father's death my mother and my brothers were starving. When the Master met Annada Guha one day, he said to him: Narendra's father has died. His family is in a state of great privation. It would be good if his friends helped him now with money.

After Annada had left I scolded him. I said, 'Why did you say all those things to him?' Thus, rebuked, he wept and said, 'Alas! for your sake I could beg from door to door.'

He tamed us by his love. Don't you think so?

M.: There is not the slightest doubt about it. His love was utterly unselfish.

Narendra: One day when I was alone with him he said something to me. Nobody else was present. Please don't repeat it to anyone here.

M.: No, I shall not. What did he say?

Narenara: He said, 'It is not possible for me to

exercise occult powers; but I shall do so through you. What do you say?' 'No,' I replied, 'you can't do that.'

I used to laugh at his words. You must have heard all these things from him. I told him that his visions of God were all hallucinations of his mind.

He said to me: 'I used to climb to the roof of the kuthi and cry, "O devotees, where are you all? Come to me, O devotees! I am about to die. I shall certainly die if I do not see you." And the Divine Mother told me, "The devotees will come." You see, everything is turning out to be true.'

What else could I say? I kept quiet.

One day he closed the door of his room and said to Devendra Babu and Girish Babu, referring to me: He will not keep his body if he is told who he is.

M.: Yes, we have heard that. Many a time he repeated the same thing to us, too. Once you came to know about your true Self in Nirvikalpa Samadhi at the Cossipore garden house. Isn't that true?

Narendra: Yes. In that experience I felt that I had no body. I could see only my face. The Master was in the upstairs room. I had that experience downstairs. I was weeping. I said: What has happened to me? The elder Gopal went to the Master's room and said: Narendra is crying.

When I saw the Master he said to me: Now you have known. But I am going to keep the key with me.

I said to him: What is it that happened to me?

Turning to the devotees, he said: He will not keep his body if he knows who he is. But I have put a veil over his eyes.

One day he said to me: You can see Krishna in your heart if you want. I replied: I don't believe in Krishna or any such nonsense! (*Both M. and Narendra laugh.*)

I used to follow my own whims in everything I did. The Master never interfered. You know that I became a member of the Sadharan Brahmo Samaj.

M.: Yes, I know that.

Narendra: The Master knew that women attended the meetings of the Brahmo Samaj. A man cannot meditate with women sitting in front of him; therefore he criticized the meditation of the Brahmo Samaj. But he didn't object to my going there.

M.: You have greater strength of mind. That is why the Master didn't prevent your going to the Samaj.

Narendra: I have attained my present state of mind as a result of much suffering and pain. You have not passed through any such suffering. I now realize that without trials and tribulation one cannot resign oneself to God and depend on Him absolutely.

8 *April* 1887

It was evening. Incense was burnt before the

pictures of gods and goddesses and the evening service was performed.

M. and Narendra were pacing the veranda and recalling old times.

Narendra: I did not believe in anything.

M.: You mean the forms of God?

Narendra: At first I did not accept most of what the Master said. One day he asked me: Then why do you come here? I replied: I come here to see you, not to listen to you.

M.: What did he say to that?

Narendra: He was very much pleased.

9 *April* 1887

Narendra was recounting to M. his various experiences with Sri Ramakrishna.

Narendra: At Cossipore he transmitted his power to me. But you must not tell this to anybody here. Give me your promise.

M.: There is a special purpose in his transmission of power to you. He will accomplish much work through you. One day the Master wrote on a piece of paper: Naren will teach people.

Narendra: But I said to him: I won't do any such thing. Thereupon he said: Your very bones will do it.

(From *The Gospel of Sri Ramakrishna*)

*   *   *

Ramakrishna used to. see a long white thread

proceeding out of himself. At the end would be a mass of light. This mass would open, and within it he would see the Mother with a Vina. Then She would begin to play; and as She played, he would see the music turning into birds and animals and worlds and arrange themselves. Then She would stop playing and they would all disappear. The light would grow less and less distinct till it was just a luminous mass, the string would grow shorter and shorter, and the whole would be absorbed into himself again. And as Swami told this, he said: 'Oh, what weird scenes things bring before me, the weirdest scenes of my whole life! Perfect silence, broken only by the cries of the jackals, in the darkness under the great tree at Dakshineswar. Night after night we sat there, the whole night through, and he talked to me, when I was a boy.' (*Reminiscences of Swami Vivekananda*, p. 286)

Behind all these manifold experiences of Ramakrishna, binding them into one great life, was always the determination to serve mankind. Vivekananda spoke of him in after years as 'writing on the ground' during the hours of darkness in the agony of his prayer that he might return to earth again, even as a dog, if only he might aid a single soul. (*The Master as I Saw Him*, pp. 336-37)

Another experience that he could never forget, was his glimpse of Sri Ramakrishna, in the week succeeding his death. It was night. He, and one other were sitting outside the house at Cossipore, talking, no doubt, of that loss of which their hearts at the moment were so full. Their Master had left them, only some few days before. Suddenly, the Swami saw a shining form enter the garden, and draw near to them. 'What was that? What was that?' said his friend, in a hoarse whisper, a few minutes later. It had been one of those rare cases in which an apparition is seen by two persons at once. (*The Master as I Saw Him*, p. 355)

Once after a lecture he came up to a small group of us and said, *apropos* of some object that had been opened up, 'I have a superstition—it is nothing, you know, but a personal superstition!—that the same soul who came once as Buddha came afterwards as Christ.' And then, lingering on the point of departure, he drifted into talk of his 'old Master', of whom we then heard for the first time and of the girl who, wedded and forgotten, gave her husband his freedom with tears. His voice had sunk lower, as he talked, till the tones had become dreamlike. But finally, almost in soliloquy, he shook off the mood that had stolen upon him, saying with a long breath, 'Yes, yes! these things have been and they will again be. Go in peace, my daughter, thy faith hath made thee whole!' (*The Master as I Saw Him*, p. 32)

There were many stories current amongst the monks, of persons who had come to Dakshineswar during the lifetime of their Master, and being touched by his hand, went immediately into Samadhi. In many cases, nothing more was known of the visitants than this. This was notably true of a certain woman, who had driven to the temple and of whom Sri Ramakrishna had said at once that she was 'a fragment of the Madonnahood of the worlds'. He had offered salutation to this guest, in the name of the Mother, throwing flowers on her feet and burning incense before her, and she, as was not perhaps surprising, had passed immediately into the deepest Samadhi. From this, however, to everyone's surprise, it had proved most difficult to recall her. It was two or three hours before she awoke from her ecstasy, and when this happened her whole appearance, it is said, was as that of one who had been intoxicated. Much relieved that all was ending thus well, however, for it had been feared that her Samadhi might last longer, and her family, wherever they were, feel justly disturbed—all lent their aid to the departure of the stranger from the temple, and none had the forethought to make a single inquiry as to her name or abode. She never came again. Thus her memory became like some beautiful legend, treasured in the Order as witness to the worship of Sri Ramakrishna for gracious and noble wifehood and motherhood. Had he not said of this woman, 'a fragment of the eternal Madonna-hood'?.... 'Was it a joke,' he [Swamiji] said, 'that Ramakrishna Paramahamsa should touch a life?

Of course he made new men and new women of these who came to him, even in these fleeting contacts!' (*The Master as I Saw Him*, pp. 182-84)

At lunch on Friday, Swami talked about Sri Ramakrishna. He abused himself for being filled and poisoned with the Western reaction of those days, so that he was always looking and questioning whether this man was 'Holy' or not. After six years he came to understand that he was 'Holy', because he had become *identified with holiness*. (*Reminiscences of Swami Vivekananda*, p. 283)

It was our last afternoon at Almora that we heard the story of the fatal illness of Sri Ramakrishna. Dr. Mahendra Lal Sarkar had been called in, and had pronounced the disease to be cancer of the throat, leaving the young disciples with many warnings as to its infectious nature. Half an hour later, 'Naren', as he then was, came in and found them huddled together, discussing the dangers of the case. He listened to what they had been told, and then, looking down, saw at his feet the cup of gruel that had been partly taken by Sri Ramakrishna and which must have contained in it, the germs of the fatal discharges of mucus and pus, as it came out in his baffled attempts to swallow the thing, on account of the stricture of the food-passage in the throat. He picked it up, and drank from it, before them all. Never was the infection of cancer mentioned amongst the disciples again. (*Notes of Some Wanderings*, p. 46)

But it was not only the historic authenticity of the personality of Buddha that held him spellbound. Another factor, at least as powerful, was the spectacle of the constant tallying of his own Master's life, lived before his eyes, with this world-attested story of twenty-five centuries before. In Buddha, he saw Ramakrishna Paramahamsa: in Rama-krishna, he saw Buddha.

In a flash this train of thought was revealed, one day when he was describing the scene of the death of Buddha. He told how the blanket had been spread for him beneath the tree, and how the Blessed One had lain down, 'resting on his right side, like a lion', to die, when suddenly there came to him one who ran for instruction. The disciples would have treated the man as an intruder, maintaining peace at any cost about their Master's death-bed, but the Blessed One overheard, and saying, 'No, no! He who was sent (the Tathagata) is ever ready,' he raised himself on his elbow, and taught. This happened four times, and then, and then only, Buddha held himself free to die....

The immortal story went on to its end. But to one who listened, the most significant moment had been that in which the teller paused—at his own words 'raised himself on his elbow and taught,'—and said, in brief parenthesis, 'I saw this, you know in the case of Ramakrishna Paramahamsa!' And there rose before the mind the story of one, destined to learn from that Teacher, who had travelled a hundred miles, and arrived at Cossipore only when he lay dying. Here also the disciples would have refused admission, but Sri Ramakrishna intervened, insisting on receiving the new-comer, and teaching him. (*The Master as I Saw Him*, pp. 254-56)

REFERENCES

The Complete Works of Swami Vivekananda

The references to the *Complete Works* (in the editions shown below) are indicated by the volume number in roman numerals and page number in arabic numerals.

Volume I	..	Thirteenth Edition, 1970
Volume II	..	Eleventh Edition, 1968
Volume III	..	Tenth Edition, 1970
Volume IV	..	Ninth Edition, 1966
Volume V	..	Ninth Edition, 1970
Volume VI	..	Eighth Edition, 1968
Volume VII	..	Seventh Edition, 1969
Volume VIII	..	Fourth Edition, 1964

Reminiscences of Swami Vivekananda: Second Edition, 1964
   By His Eastern and Western Admirers
The Master As I Saw Him: Ninth Edition, 1963
   By Sister Nivedita
Notes of Some Wanderings with the Swami Vivek-ananda: Fourth Edition, 1957
   By Sister Nivedita
Ramakrishna and His Disciples: Second Edition, 1969
   By Christopher Isherwood
The Gospel of Sri Ramakrishna: American Edition, 1942
   By 'M': Translated by Swami Nikhilananda
Sri Ramakrishna The Great Master: Madras Math, 1952
   By Swami Saradananda: Translated by Swami Jagadananda
Nivedita Lokamata (Bengali): First Edition, 1968
   By Sri Sankariprasad Basu

The Life of Ramakrishna

By Romain Rolland

A fascinating and unvarnished account of the life of the greatest prophet of the modern age by one of the masterminds of the West; a critical appreciation of the finest flower of the Indian culture; also a masterpiece of literary art, enriched with a wealth of details.

Pp. 244   Price: Rs. 45

Ramakrishna and His Disciples

By Christopher Isherwood

In this new biography of the great master, Mr. Isherwood approaches Sri Ramakrishna with love and devotion, just like any Hindu, and at the same time, deals with his subject in the scientific spirit of a Western investigator.

Pp. 348   Price: Rs. 40

Life of Sri Ramakrishna

With a Foreword by Mahatma Gandhi

A comprehensive chronological account of the Master's wonderful life, the only authorized version of its kind in English.

Mahatma Gandhi says in the *Foreword*, " The Story of Ramakrishna Paramahamsa's life is a story of religion in practice. His life enables us to see God face to face. No one can read the story of his life without being convinced that God alone is real, and that all else is an illusion."

Pp. 620   Price: Rs. 60

For a detailed list of books write to:

The Manager
Advaita Ashrama
5 Dehi Entally Road
Kolkata 700 014